THE BARE HISTORY OF LEEK

BEING

THE BARE BONES OF THE HISTORY OF LEEK

COMPILED BY

PHILIP BROUGH

Published by Curlew Press for the author

ISBN: 978-1-9161044-9-5

Print: Hobbs the Printers Ltd, Totton, Hampshire SO40 3XW

Design: Mark Titterton

Captions

Front cover: Derby Street, Leek. Photograph by Nigel Maycock

Back cover: Plan of Leek, 1838 - copied (1899) by R. Ewan

DEDICATION

I wish to dedicate this book to all those who have assisted me in changing a document into articles and articles into a book; especially all of those past and present historians of our wonderful town whose works I have devoured over many years.

THE BAREBONE'S HISTORY OF LEEK

BEING

THE BARE BONES OF THE HISTORY OF LEEK

COMPILED BY

PHILIP BROUGH

Why the "**BAREBONES HISTORY OF LEEK**"?

Quite simply because I believe that there is a need for a concise, strictly chronological history of Leek, rather than one dealing with specific aspects of it.

Where did the title originate? The answer is also simple:

(1) Any schoolchild who has been taught anything at all about the period of English History surrounding the Civil War will remember, with amusement, the "*Barebones Parliament*" of Charles I, so called after one of its members "*Praise-God Barebone*". (The fact that his name was "Barbon" did not get in the way of a good historical story!)

(2) This booklet does not attempt to be an exhaustive history of Leek, but will attempt to be a chronological list of the basic facts relating to the history of Leek. In essence, it attempts to set down the "*bare bones*" of Leek's history; leaving it to others, more talented, to flesh out the simple skeleton given here.

The booklet arises out of a number of lectures that the compiler gave to the Leek U3A in 2008, which in turn were based on notes that he had compiled over a number of years. He was born and bred in Leek – a member of an old Leek family. Like so many others, the call of a career dictated that, at the age of twenty-one, he moved away. He was lucky enough to be able to return to North Staffordshire on retirement.

Whilst he was away, again like so many others, circumstances dictated that barely a thought was given to the town of Leek. It was necessary to earn a living and to make a new life, in a new town, in a new part of the country; six times in fact! But there comes a time in the life of most "exiles" when their attention returns to their childhood; to the places that they knew and loved when young; to old friends and school friends. This is when they buy every book available about the town and its history and read them avidly. The compiler has always been in the custom of making notes when reading such books. With the coming of computers, it became an easy task to maintain those notes in chronological order. Those notes formed the basis of the lectures that, in turn, formed the basis of this booklet.

To his shame, he must confess to being a bad note-taker; he did not make a note of his sources, for the notes were only intended to be read by him! This is a pity for it means that he cannot give credit to those others who deserve it. He is only too aware of his own shortcomings, for there are many who know far more about aspects of Leek than he does. His excuse is that he is a barrister and not a private detective; he merely reproduces, in a different form, the works of others. Like Isaac Newton, he realises that he is *standing on the shoulders of giants*". He defends himself by using the old adage – "*to read one book is plagiarism but to read many books is research.*" He acknowledges his debt to other, far better, writers and researchers.

INTRODUCTION

Let us begin at the beginning, or rather even before the beginning, and consider what Leek was like in its very earliest of days. We can get an idea from the underlying rocks upon which the town stands. Warm inland seas produce sand; and sand produces both sandstone and millstone grit, depending upon the pressure applied. Leek stands on those two types of stone. The millstone grit may be seen at the Roches (I personally prefer this spelling to the alternative "Roaches" because they are rocks and not fish), Wetley Rocks etc. The sandstone may be seen in Broad Street, Mill Street and Cheddleton Road and the two types of rock meet in a line running, approximately, down the centre of Derby Street.

To picture Leek before man arrived, it is necessary to imagine the area of St Edward's Church, Church Street, St Edward Street and the Market Place. Then, in your imagination, remove those streets and the buildings in them and, where the "lip" to the top of Mill Street now is, imagine a small cliff. Now imagine a stream of pure water, flowing out of an outcrop of rock just below the very top of the hill and running down what is now St Edward Street. Imagine the land between Derby Street and Stockwell Street sloping gently down to a marsh where the Monument now stands, with water percolating into it from the land situated between the present Buxton Road and Ashbourne Road. Two streams emerged from this marsh. One of them flowed down what is now Ball Haye Street and Ball Haye Road to turn left into the present Brough Park and eventually flow into the River Churnet at Abbey Green Road. The other stream flowed southwards, down what is now Brook Street. Now imagine the whole area covered with trees; and there you have Leek, as it was before mankind arrived.

St Edward's Street

Crosses in St Edward's Church churchyard

Leek has been described as "*a town on a hill in a valley*", and when early man decided to settle down, this is the type of place that they would have been looking for. They needed sites with certain specific requirements. Firstly, a hilltop: somewhere that is easier to defend; secondly, access to clean water; and thirdly, welldrained land to clear and cultivate. Leek had them all. The hilltop is plain to see, for from the site of St Edward's Church the land drops away in every direction; the water flowing from the top of the hill has already been mentioned, and the land to cultivate slopes gently down from the hilltop and along the land that abuts what is now West Street and Wellington Street. The site of the Westwood Recreation ground – in fact, all of the ridge between Broad Street and Mill Street – was dedicated to strip farming and the fields were known *as "the Dragon's Crofts"*. There is thus every indication that Leek was an inhabited site from the earliest of days and that the first dwellings adjoined the religious site at the top of hill, and were also adjacent to the stream.

The town was also defended by water for it is almost completely surrounded by the River Churnet and the stream that once flowed from the marsh (on the site of the Monument) down Ball Haye Street, Ball Haye Road and across the bottom of Brough Park (where the lake used to be) and so into the Churnet. The water defences were completed by the other stream flowing out of the marsh and down Brook Street to join the town stream at the bottom of St Edward Street (formerly Spout Street).

Leek is a magical place. To our early ancestors, it had a great religious importance before it was inhabited. This is proved by the simple fact that there are no houses on the highest point of the town, the site of St Edward's Church. In Leek we have a religious site that has never been built upon except for the church. It would have been a circular site because most pagan temples were circular, and the position at the very top of a hill would automatically suggest a round pagan temple; not a building, but a site. That there was a temple on that site cannot be proved, but three factors would indicate that there was:

The first Christian Church in Leek was built on that site and Christian churches were always built, where possible, on the site of a pagan temple, in order that the converts could attend the same site for their religious services as they had before.

The fact that it is from this site that our forebears would notice the double sunset. The sun played such a prominent part in their everyday life that a place where the sun sets twice during the course of an evening must have been very important to them. If, as has been suggested, the double sunset was not visible then, there would still have been a magnificent view of the setting sun.

Then there is the often overlooked fact of the stream of pure water emanating from the top of this hill. Springs are to be found in many places, and where they are found they often had a religious significance – village well dressings, for example. But springs usually emerge from the ground at the bottom of hills. Here in Leek, we have a spring which emerges from the ground at the very top of a hill.

The great importance of this spring is reflected in the fact that the very name of the town is derived from it. The name of "Leek" derives from "Lec" and that, in turn, is derived from the Old English *hlec*, meaning a place from which water flows. "Leek" and "Leak" are, etymologically speaking, the same word. Why is Leek water different from any other water? Because of where it originates: at the top of a hill!

Think for a moment. Common sense tells us that water does not flow from the top of a hill. Where it does must be a "magical" place. The water flowed out from what is now the churchyard of St Edward's Church. A drinking fountain, no longer operative, was set into the wall in the place from whence the water used to flow. Any water that would flow from there today would flow down Mill Street, but before the cliff was demolished and that road was built, it would have flowed down St Edward Street, (originally Spout Street) and via what is now Broad Street, into the River Churnet.

Church Fountain

Later, when a gentry became established, they would need larger houses, close to the existing houses but removed from them. These would have been built on the opposite side of the Market Place, where the Red Lion now stands.

Leek's first suburb (for want of a better name) – the place where people chose to live once the area around the church had all been occupied – was in the present Moorhouse Street area. These houses were built on the moor side on the town, and were separated from the actual town by the marsh that lay at the lower end of Derby Street. Naturally, in time, this marsh was drained and the streams stopped flowing.

Others, far cleverer persons than I, have found traces of our forebears. Dating from the Neolithic, Bronze and Iron Ages, the Leek Trackway has been traced from Waterhouses, Waterfall Cross, Standing Stone Farm, Bottomhouse, Lower Lady Meadows, Combes Brook, Cooks Lane, Bradnop, Low Hill, through Leek, on to the Cloud and off across the Cheshire Plain.

When the Romans arrived in England, they were responsible for the Leek to Buxton Road. Through the town of Leek, it ran from the Moss Rose, down the Organ Ground, Fountain Street, Derby Street, Strangman Street, The Walks, Newcastle Road and Wallbridge. The name "Wall" is always a good indication of a Roman presence, and they built a bridge across the Churnet at Wallbridge, together with a fortress to protect the crossing. The documentation of Dieulacres Abbey mentions a road to Wallbridge called the "*via Castella*" – the road to the castle.

In the late 600s, Leek formed part of the AngloSaxon Kingdom of Mercia. Tribute was paid to the King of Mercia, in kind, not coin, and a large barn was built to accommodate the accumulated rents paid in corn and cattle etc. The probable site for this building is where the old Vicarage now stands, between the Church and the Market Place. There are (the remains of) four Saxon crosses in the church and churchyard.

All of these indicate that Leek was an inhabited site from the very earliest of days. We are indeed fortunate that those early citizens of the town engaged in trade with local farmers and itinerant merchants, for they left a large open space for the market, and it remains the Market Place to this day. It was originally much bigger than it is today and stretched from the Red Lion to St Edward Street. The church then stood in its rightful position, at the top of the market square. Merchants' stalls were erected on the side of the market square, later becoming permanent buildings and streets, which retained the name of their original use and became Sheepmarket and Custard Street (where Costard apples were sold), which was later changed to Stanley Street.

Here, then, we have the earliest Leek dwellings, gradually spreading out along St Edward Street, Church Street, Sheepmarket and Stanley Street. Over the centuries, the town developed into what it is today. This account will set out the milestones in its development.

Where possible, the compiler has avoided words such as "about" or "circa", but he does ask the reader to bear in mind that not all dates given are exact and that many, particularly the early ones, are estimations. Secondly, as he often quotes, "*a spy is only as good as his source of information.*" It often occurs that two or more sources give two or more different dates for an event. Where he has found that this has happened, he has opted for the date that he thinks is the most likely. He fully accepts that he may have chosen the wrong one!

The rest of these articles will be in strict note form. They will provide the bare bones of the history of the town of Leek. The flesh will have to be applied by others with more skill than he.

He has taken the liberty of inserting markers; that is to say, events of national or of world importance. These are designed to enable the reader to mentally date a local event and appreciate what was happening in the country and in the world at that time.

Here then is

THE BAREBONES HISTORY OF LEEK

OR

THE BARE BONES OF THE HISTORY OF LEEK

THE ELEVENTH CENTURY AND BEFORE

100 – The Roman road between Leek and Buxton has been established. It continued south through Cheddleton, Blythe Bridge, Hilderstone, and Stafford to join Watling Street at Pennocrucium (Penkridge).

600 – There is a medieval road running east from Leek along what is now Fountain Street and turning northeast over Leek Moor into Tittesworth. It was part of a medieval road, called the Earl's Way, which linked the estates of the Earls of Chester. That part of the road to the east of Leek formed the medieval road that ran at least as far as Waterhouses. To the northwest of Leek, the Earl's Way followed the Macclesfield road through Rudyard to Rushton Spencer, where it turned west through Rushton James to Congleton.

800 – There are the remains of several preNorman crosses in the church and churchyard. A rectangularshafted cross south of the church was set up there after lying for several years in three pieces against the east wall of the churchyard. It has a fragment of runic inscription and may date from the early 9th century. The roundshafted cross at the southeast of church is a particularly fine and well-preserved example of its type, dating perhaps from the later 10th century. Inside the church are the remains of the wheelhead of a cross and also stone from a rectangular shaft with a carving, perhaps depicting Christ carrying the Cross.

980 – A church is built in Leek on the present site of St Edward's Church.

1013 – **The Danes become the masters of England**

1042 – **Edward the Confessor**

1066 – **The Battle of Hastings – William I – The Conqueror**

1085 – The town of Leek is a Royal possession.

1086 – **Domesday Book**

"The King holds Lec – Earl Alfgar held it – the son of Leofric, Duke of Mercia – 1 hide 'with appendages' + 2 ploughs – population 15 villagers + 13 smallholders with 6 ploughs" – "Leek manor has 12 plough teams – 15 villani and 13 bordars with 6 teams – 3 acres of meadow, and woodland measured 4 leagues in length and 4 in breadth".

The value of the manor has increased from £4 in 1066 to £5.

Leek has a population of 28.

1093 – Leek is granted by the King to Hugh, Earl of Chester. He is known as "Hugh the Fat" and is so large that he can hardly walk. When he dies, he is buried in the Chapter House of Chester Cathedral. The endowments given to Chester Abbey by the Earl include all the tithes from his manor of Leek.

1096 – The First Crusade

THE TWELFTH CENTURY

1100 – **Henry I**

1135 – **King Stephen**

1150 – Ranulf, Earl of Chester, has a mill at Leek, presumably a watermill on the River Churnet, at the bottom of Mill Street.

A Borough Charter, granted by his grandson, Earl Ranulf de Blundeville, stipulates that the burgesses (that is, freemen and not serfs) of Leek are obliged to grind their corn at his mill "*immediately after that which shall be in the hopper*", paying a toll of one twentieth of the grain brought in for grinding.

1154 – **Henry II – Adrian IV, the only "English" Pope**

1170 – **Thomas à Becket assassinated**

Hugh of Kevelioc, Earl of Chester, issues charters at Leek, showing that he is actually living here for at least part of the year. He lives in a house that would have stood on the site of the present Red Lion, in the Market Place. It was the custom for members of the nobility to have a number of large houses scattered about their domains. In fact, this was a practical necessity. In those days, ways of preserving foodstuffs were very limited and with their large number of retainers it would not be long before all of the food in a locality had been consumed and the privies were full to overflowing. The nobleman, his family and his retainers would then simply move on to another house. By the time they returned, the house would have been cleaned and refreshed and the food reserves replenished. This custom still prevails, although the reason for it no longer exists. The Royal Family, for example, still has its set seasons with the late summer and early autumn being spent at Balmoral; autumn being spent in London, at Buckingham Palace and Windsor; Christmas and part of the winter at Sandringham; spring in London again for "The Season" – the Garter Ceremony, Ascot, Henley Royal Regatta and the Royal Garden Parties.

1180 – The manor of Leek is in the hands of the King because of the minority of Ranulf, the Earl of Chester. Cattle farming is becoming an important part of the economy of the district of Leek.

1181 – Hugh of Kevelioc, the Earl of Chester, dies at Leek.

1183 – Thirtytwo cows are bought in to complete the stocking of the manor.

1185 – Beekeeping is important, with five shillings being raised by the sale of honey from the manor.

1189 – **Richard I – The Lionheart**

1199 – **King John**

THE THIRTEENTH CENTURY

1207 – Ranulf, Earl of Chester grants a charter to "*my free burgesses dwelling in my borough of Leek.*" They are to be as free as "*the freer burgesses*" of any other borough in Staffordshire. Each is to have half an acre attached to his dwelling and one acre in the fields – with a right to timber and firewood in Leek forest and common of pasture for all cattle in Leek manor. The burgesses are to pay no rent for the first three years and thereafter twelve pence each year. They are also to be quit of all amercements (fees or charges) relating to Leek. They are free to give or sell their burgages to anyone other than religious – subject to a toll of four pence. (The ban on transfers of land to religious bodies was because such tenure included an obligation to serve the Lord as a soldier in time of war. A transfer of land to the Church meant that this right was lost – the land went into a "dead hand" – a "*mort gage*", the origin of our modern word "mortgage".) They are to be exempted from pannage dues (the right to pasture pigs in the forest) in the manor – and they are granted privileged grinding at the Earl's mills. The burgesses are exempted from tolls throughout Cheshire on all goods except salt at the wiches.

King John confirms to Earl Ranulf the right to hold a weekly market and an annual sevenday fair. The annual fair is to take place beginning three days before the Feast of St Edward (20 June, the Feast of the Second Translation of Edward the Martyr, or 13 October, the Feast of Translation of Edward the Confessor).

1208 – King John seals Leek's Charter.

1210 – Ranulf de Blundeville, the Earl of Chester, issues a Charter in Leek which stipulates that those coming to the market and the fair should pay only the same toll as is paid in other free markets of Staffordshire.

Settlement is taking place in the area of the present Ballington Wood.

Ralph of Baliden is a tenant in the fee of Leek.

1214 – The Earl of Chester founds Dieulacres Abbey, beside the Churnet, a mile north of the town, at Cholpesdale. It later has granges at Swythamley, Birchall, Westwood, Roche Grange, Foker and Easing.

The parish priest is "*living near the church*".

1215 – **Magna Carta** – Leek's Second Charter granted

1220 – **Henry III** – The town has developed as a commercial centre.

Moorhouse, to the southeast, is an occupied site. It is Leek's first suburb, being situated on the "other side" of the marsh where the Monument now stands.

Market Place

There are 80½ burgages in Leek.

The Earl receives 20 shillings from tolls from the market and the fair.

1222 – Leek Church is granted to Dieulacres Abbey. The rectory is held by the monks until the Dissolution. The grant is confirmed by William Cornhill, the Bishop of Coventry. He institutes the monks into the vacant church. The bishop fixes its value at twenty marks (one mark = weight of eight ounces of silver). His confirmation mentions the existence of dependent chapels.

1223 – Earl Ranulf has granted the mill to the monks of Dieulacres.

1226 – The dependent chapels of Dieulacres are named as Cheddleton, Ipstones and Horton in a further confirmation made by the Bishop of Coventry, Alexander Stavensby.

1230 – Another route from Leek to Macclesfield is recorded. It ran via Abbey Green and Gun, and entered Cheshire at Danebridge.

The Bishop, taking compassion on the poverty of Dieulacres Abbey, and at the petitioning of Ranulf de Blundeville, Earl of Chester, grants to them the Church of Leek and its chapels.

Richard Patrick is the Vicar of Leek.

1232 – The right to the market and fair pass to Dieulacres Abbey, along with the manor, but the Abbot's renewal of the Borough Charter makes no mention of the payment of tolls.

Ranulf states that his bailiffs would exact from the men of the manor "suit at mill" on behalf of the monks and the customary work on the mill and its pool. (This is the compulsory requirement that all corn must be ground at the mill and that the monks could call upon the townspeople to carry out repairs.)

The Abbot renews the Borough Charter, including the clause relating to grinding of the burgesses' corn at the mill. The monks of Dieulacres Abbey renewed the charter of the Earl of Chester a short time after Earl Ranulf's grant of the manor to the Abbey. The renewal omits the clauses covering the rights to timber, firewood and pasture, exemption from pannage and the tolls payable at the market and the fair. The twelve pence rent is to be paid in two parts: sixpence on the Feast of St Edward in the summer (20 June) and sixpence at Martinmas (11 November). The ban on the conveyance of burgages to the religious is modified to allow a conveyance to Dieulacres itself: Ranulf, Earl of Chester, grants the manor of Leek to the monks of Dieulacres Abbey, along with his heart for burial. The King confirms the grant the day before Ranulf's death. Ranulf's nephew and heir, John Scot, later grants to the monks the homage (an acknowledgement that the town is under the power of the monastery) and the services belonging to the manor which he has initially retained.

1241 – Leek has a vicar with a deacon.

The advowson (the right to appoint the priest) remained with Dieulacres Abbey until the Dissolution.

1244 – The monks of Trentham give the monks of Dieulacres permission to build a bridge at Wallbridge on the Newcastle Road and also free access for waggons and carts across Trentham Priory's land at Wall in Longsdon.

1246 – Earl Ranulf has granted to the monks of Dieulacres all rights in the land at Birchall. The monks have established a grange there (a grange was originally a granary but later became a farmhouse with buildings) and possibly another at Westwood. An estate has been granted to Dieulacres Abbey by Flora, the daughter of William of Cockshut.

1250 – A burgage exists at Wallbridge.

1250 – Castle Way (*via castelli*), the road to Wallbridge, is mentioned

1253 – Linen is first manufactured in England

1272 – Edward I

1275 – Marco Polo visits China

1281 – There is mention of a Court being held in Leek.

There is a mention of "*Elyot le quarehour*" (Elliot the Quarrier), who formerly held land near Leek churchyard. This indicates quarrying is taking place in the area.

Church Brook, later Ball Haye Brook, is known as "Kyrkebroke" (Kirkbrook).

The Church in Leek is, by this date, dedicated to St Edward.

1288 – There is a "composition of the church" (i.e. all deeds and charters are brought together into one single document) but there is no mention of the glebe.

St Edwards Church

The Bishop settles a dispute between the Vicar of Leek and monks by ordering that the vicar is to have all of the annual oblations, plus the customary Lent offerings at Candlemas, plus the casual perquisites, the small tithes, the tithe of hay from Endon, six marks a year from the monks plus the house by the church *"which it is customary for the vicar to have"*. In return, the vicar has the duty of providing priests to serve the dependent chapels.

1290 – Land at Upper Tittesworth is held "by suit" (i.e. by petition) at Leek Court twice a year.

1291 – Dieulacres Abbey establishes a grange at Westwood, one mile west of the town. Westwood Grange consists of two carucates (a carucate is as much land as a team of oxen could plough in one season) worth £1 year, plus 6s. 8d. a year from the sale of meadow.

The Abbey farms out the manor of Leek for £10 6s. 4d.

The right to insist that burgesses use the Earl's mill is valued at £1.

Leek Church with its dependent chapel (either Horton or Ipstones) is valued at £28.

1293 – The Abbot of Dieulacres as Lord of the Manor claims "*infangthief and right of gallows*" (i.e. the right to catch, try and execute (or fine) any thief within the boundary of the town).

1293 – William of Cockshut's greatgrandson, Thomas, son of Robert of Olynleye, (Hollinhay at Longsdon?) claims toft (a homestead) and 120 acres at Westwood as William's heir, but the jury upholds the Abbot's claim that William had enfeoffed (granted) Flora with the land before he died and that she therefore had the right to dispose of it.

The Abbot of Dieulacres claims frankpledge as the Lord of Leek, in succession to Ranulf de Blundeville, Earl of Chester. (Frankpledge was a mutual law enforcement by which each member of a tithing area was responsible for the actions of all other members.)

1297 – The Church of Leek burns down together with the whole town.

THE FOURTEENTH CENTURY

1300 – The convergence of roads on the northwest, south-west and east sides of the town and the pattern of property boundaries have suggested to some that the medieval town may have had a hard boundary, perhaps an earth bank pierced with gates.

The boundary of Leek and Lowe township is formed by various watercourses: the Churnet on the northwest and west, Leek Brook on the south, and Kniveden Brook.

St Edward's Church serves a large parish which includes the dependent chapels at Cheddleton, Horton, Ipstones, Meerbrook, Onecote and Rushton Spencer.

1306 – St Edward's Church is rebuilt. The Church nave is long and narrow, reproducing its earlier proportions, and fully aisled on both sides. Part of the western respond (a half-pillar attached to a wall in order to support an arch) of the north aisle remains and is evidence that the aisle formerly extended the full length of nave. The north arcade has octagonal piers, three of which survived until the early 19th century.

1307 – **Edward II**

1314 – **Battle of Bannockburn**

1315 – Lowe Hill has become an inhabited area.

1315/– **Non-stop floods. No corn. Hay too wet to harvest.**
16/17

1318 – King Edward II, two archbishops, nine bishops plus "many magnates" attend a meeting on 7 August between Leek and Horton to reconcile the differences between the King and Thomas, Earl of Lancaster.

1320 – The fair is still held around the feast of St Edward.

There is a record of a Small Court being held at Leek.

One of St Edward's feasts (20 June) is appointed as the day on which the burgesses of Leek have to pay the first half of their rent.

1327 – **Edward III**

Eight people are assessed for tax in Leek *"cum membris"* (together with their families and servants) and fourteen in Lowe.

1330 – Several people are living at Wallbridge.

1331 – **First record of weaving in England**

1332 – There is mention of three bondmen being at Wildecroft in the Earl of Chester's fee of Leek. Wildecroft is probably Woodcroft.

1333 – There are thirty-three assessed for tax in Leek and Lowe.

1337 – **Richard II**

1340 – Each of the five townships making up the manor has formed a tithing represented by one frankpledge at a twiceyearly view.

A chaplain is celebrating daily at the altar of St Mary in the Leek church. He holds the messuage (dwelling and adjoining land appropriated to a household) and twelve acres in Leek for life by the grant of William, the Vicar of Leek.

Besides Leek and Lowe, the manor of Leek includes Heaton, Leekfrith, Rushton Spencer and Tittesworth. A tithing (land held subject to the payment of tithes) exists called Woodcroft.

1341 – William, the Vicar of Leek, receives a Royal Licence to use property for the permanent endowment of a chantry at the altar.

1345 – The monks of Dieulacres own the manor of Birchall Grange.

1346 – **Battle of Crecy**

1348 – **Founding of the Order of the Garter**

1351 – **Black Death**

1399 – **Henry IV**

1379 – Abbot William of Lichfield is charged with being an accessory to the murder of John Warton of Leek.

THE FIFTEENTH CENTURY

1413 – Henry V

1415 – Battle of Agincourt

1422 – Henry VI

1429 – Several officials are elected at the Great Court held in January: the constable, the ale taster, two meat tasters and a bailiff (*catchpoll*) with an associate (*socius*).

A tithing exists called Lowe.

1430 – The road to the south, from Leek to Cheddleton, is described as being part of the highway from Leek to Stafford.

The bridge on the road to Congleton, where it crosses the River Churnet, is known as "*Conyngre bridge*", after a nearby rabbit warren.

1431 – Joan of Arc burnt at the stake

1439 – A gallows stands "*at the end of the town*" – probably at the top of Mill Street. It is stated to have always stood there.

1450 – The Vicar of Leek is still in receipt of the dues stipulated in 1288 and the six marks stipend, but the payment of £15 year to the chaplains of Cheddleton, Ipstones and Horton leave him with only fourteen marks. The stipends of the chaplains are made a charge upon the rectory.

An Inquisition is held at which there is no mention of the glebe lands.

1452 – Leonardo da Vinci born

1455 – Wars of the Roses begin

1461 – Edward IV

1465 – The King bans "the hustling of stones" (bowls?)

1483 – Edward V – Richard III

1485 – Henry VII

1490 – There are twenty draught oxen at Birchall.

1492 – Columbus makes voyage to the New World

1495 – Syphilis epidemic through England

THE SIXTEENTH CENTURY

1500 – Monks are involved in arable farming at the granges, with stock farming also taking place at Birchall.

1501 – Birchall has ten draught oxen with two heifers.

1502 – Birchall has twenty draught oxen, a number of cows and 200 sheep.

At Westwood there are ten draught oxen.

1503 – **Mona Lisa painted**

A house at Moorhouse passes by marriage from the Bailey family to John Jodrell of Yeardsley, in Taxall.

1508 – Birchall has six cows "plus other animals".

1509 – **Henry VIII**

1510 – The tower of the church is remodelled and given a new top stage. The clerestory is added and the roofs of the aisles are renewed.

1512 – **Martin Luther made Doctor of Divinity**

1516 – There is a great riot at Leek when Abbot William Albyn enlists armed men to prevent the arrest of wrong-doers accused of murder.

1517 – **Luther posts his protest**

1520 – **Luther excommunicated**

1521 – **Silk manufacture introduced into France**

1530 – The burgesses are in fear for their liberties because their charter has come into the possession of Thomas Rudyard, the Lord of Rudyard Manor.

1531 – **Henry VII takes the title of "Supreme Head of the Church"**

1535 – The rectory income consists of £1 4s. 0d. rent from Leek glebe land; £18 3s. 8d. from the great tithes belonging to Leek church; £17 from other tithes; £7 5s. 4d. from the Easter Roll; and £2 6s. 8d. from offerings. The vicar receives £7 19s. 1½d. from offerings and other emoluments.

A farm at Kniveden is leased to Thomas Smith by the monks of Dieulacres Abbey.

Both Birchall and Westwood granges have been leased to the Brereton family of Westwood; Westwood Grange being known as the grange of Westwood and Woodcroft.

1536 – **Dissolution of the Monasteries starts**

1537 – By will, Edmund Washington of Leek leaves £26 13s. 4d. to the new chapel of St Catherine in Leek Church, to be used to provide stock chosen by the parish for the support of a priest to pray for the souls of Edmund's father and mother, and for their children. Edmund directs that his son William "*shall sing for me if he will as long as the stock doth last*" and that he is to be buried "*in my own form before St Catherine*".

1538 – Dissolution of the monastery of Dieulacres. The Abbot is Thomas Whitney. The Earl of Derby is the steward of the manor as well as steward of the Borough and of Dieulacres Abbey. There is a single bailiff for all of the abbey's manors. The town thereafter has its own bailiff. At the Dissolution the abbey has two watermills at Leek – one on the Churnet in Mill Street and the other at Birchall.

A fair is held in the town on the Feast of St Arnulf (18 July) and on the seven days following.

1539 – 20 October – Dieulacres is formally surrendered to the King. The property includes the Parsonage of the Church of Leek Rectory, valued at £63 4s. 8d., and also the tithe barns at Birchall Grange, at Fowlchurch Grange in Tittesworth, at Endon, and at Heaton and Longsdon.

1540 – The Grand Canyon discovered by Spanish explorers

1542 – There is one "free" tenement in Leek and Lowe. Four other tenements, including Birchall Grange, owe rent of two capons worth sixpence, one day's ploughing worth threepence, and one day's reaping worth threepene, while the fifth, Westwood Grange, owes rent of four capons, and two days of each work.

Extensive work is carried out on the chancel of the church. Fiftynine loads of stone are used and expenditure includes £2 12s. 4d. on glass "*for window*" plus £3 on plastering.

1543 – A statue of Our Lady stands in the chapel of St Mary in St Edward's Church.

1545 – The chapel of St Mary in St Edward's Church is mentioned in wills as a burial place.

1547 – Edward VI

Robert Burgh of Leekfrith leaves 20d. to "Our Lady's service" at Leek.

1548 – The church chantry has lands worth more than £2 per year net plus plate and ornaments worth ten shillings. The church has its own wardens who could dismiss the chaplain.

1548 – A twiceyearly Great Court and threeweekly Small Court is still being held with between 300 and 400 suitors attending the Great Court.

1549 – The Crown sells the Church endowments consisting of six messuages and land in Leek parish.

1550 – All or most of the surviving timberframed buildings are of the 16th or 17th century, although later encased in stone or brick. Numbers 2 and 4 Clerk Bank and the Black Swan Inn in Sheepmarket both contain cruck (roughly cut and naturally curved) frames.

Numbers 2 and 4 Church Street, on the north side of the marketplace, incorporate the remains of a 16thcentury timberframed building, whose front probably jettied (upper stories projected over the street). At the rear is another timberframed building, originally detached, which has a large fireplace and may have been the kitchen. The town is known as the manors of Leek and Frith, at that time still covering Leek and Lowe, Heaton, Leekfrith, Rushton Spencer and Tittesworth.

The Rectory of Leek is leased out to Michael Wentworth, for £52 9s. 4d. per annum.

Church Street

1551 – The tithing area is being called Leek.

1552 – The Crown grants the manors of Leek and Frith, together with the site of Dieulacres Abbey and most of the former abbey's Staffordshire property, to Sir Ralph Bagnall at a rent of £105 11s. 7½d. Birchall Grange and Westwood Grange are included in the grant of the Abbey's property to Sir Ralph Bagnall. The right to hold the market and the fair is also included. The town's borough status is lost after this grant as Sir Ralph Bagnall proceeds to deny the burgesses their rights.

1553 – Queen Mary I

St Edward's Church's two bells and a handbell, probably the sanctus bell, are sold for 12 shillings. The plate consisted of a silver chalice and paten plus a brass cross.

1555 – Tobacco imported into Spain

The burgesses assert their rights, in particular the right to dispose of their tenements as they wish and the right to collect wood in the commons of the manor.

1556 – Sir Ralph Bagnall, who is a staunch Protestant, is living in France when he is found guilty of treason in his absence.

Sir Nicholas Bagnall, to whom Sir Ralph Bagnall has conveyed his property, further conveys it to Valentine Brown.

In the church, the arcades are replaced by walls. The date on the stones (1556) in the south aisle relates to this work.

1557 – Sir Ralph Bagnall of Leek is pardoned.

1558 – Queen Elizabeth I

1559 – Queen Elizabeth gives the town tithes to "*Sir Raufe Begenalle*".

Dissolution of eighty-four burgages.

1560 – The earliest known inn is "The Swan", although this may not be the present Swan.

A "cucking stool" stands by the River Churnet, off Abbey Green Road near Broad's Bridge.

Sir Ralph Bagnall recovers his property from Valentine Brown.

The Crown grants the advowson to Sir Ralph Bagnall. It then descended with the Leek manor.

Sir Ralph Bagnall is appointed as the Sheriff of Staffordshire.

The rectory is granted to Sir Ralph Bagnall at feefarm rent of £5 3s. 0d., which is given as the value of the rectory. The grant is made in recognition of his services and in consideration of all of the money owed to him for his service in Ireland. Sir Ralph sells most of the tithes to the owners of the property on which they are due.

1562 – Thomas Smith buys a farm at Kniveden. The Smith family start to live at Kniveden farm (and remained there until 1845).

1563 – A tithe barn exists at Birchall.

Sir Ralph Bagnall conveys Birchall Grange to William Egerton of Fenton.

The jurors of the Manor Court state that the tenants may grind their corn where they please.

1565 – **Potatoes and tobacco introduced into England**

Sir Ralph Bagnall conveys the mills to Ralph Rudyard, who challenges the rights of the tenants to have their corn ground where they please.

A fishery in the River Churnet forms part of the Birchall Grange estate.

1566 – Queen Elizabeth grants the reversion (the right to future ownership) of the rectory and chapels of the rectory to Sir Ralph Bagnall for £51 3s. 0d. per annum

1568 – **Mary, Queen of Scots flees to England**

The first known schoolmaster in town is John Lumford. He is a graduate.

1569 – Ball Hay Brook is called "*a tributary of the Churnet*".

1572 – Rent of £105 11s. 7½d., which has been reserved by the Crown in 1552, is in arrears to the amount of £446 3s. 9d.

1575 – The spring to the south of the town, to the east of the Cheddleton road, evidently named in honour of Our Lady, is known as the Lady Wall Dale and spring.

The Cock Low is recorded as "Catteslowe". (It will be recalled that this Lowe is the great one that was situated between the Waterloo Mill and the Westwood Recreation Ground.)

Ladydale well

The Moot Hall in the town is held by a tenant and is probably the meeting place of the Borough Court.

1580 – Sir Ralph Bagnall, having sold much of his property, is succeeded by his nephew, Sir Henry Bagnall.

1586 – Famine in England

The inhabitants of Leek are presented (charged before) the Quarter Sessions for allowing fairs and markets to be held in the churchyard. (The Quarter Sessions were a higher court than the Petty Sessions held in the town. They consisted of the meeting of the magistrates, once a quarter, in Stafford, the place where more serious cases were tried.)

1587 – Mary, Queen of Scots executed

1588 – Spanish Armada

1589 – Four people in Leek parish are presented for absence from church. Three of them are female members of the Comberford family. (In order to strengthen the Church of England, attendance at church was enforced by law. All who failed to attend church were deemed to be "recusants" and fined.)

1590 – Two recusants are recorded in Leek.

The inclosure of the Leek field is in progress. This is a large open field which extended from the Nab Hill area and Belle Vue Road to the east side of the Cheddleton road. Piecemeal inclosure is in progress. (Gentry who had purchased Church property when the monasteries were dissolved were naturally anxious to maximise their profits and so did not hesitate to turn land which had hitherto been common land into their own property by fencing it and expelling the common people.)

1592 – Roger Banne, the Vicar of Leek from 1569 to 1619, is described as being *"skilled in sacred letters"* and *"a praiseworthy instructor of his flock"*.

1595 – Ralph Adderley of Coton in Hanbury dies and is succeeded by his son William. Westwood Grange passes to him.

1597 – Sir Henry Bagnall conveys the manors of Leek and Frith, including the rectory and the advowson, to Thomas Rudyard. The manors then descended with Rudyard Manor. The right to hold the market and the fair is included in the sale.

Red Lion

Roebuck

THE SEVENTEENTH CENTURY

1600 – The population of England and Ireland is about five million

The town of Leek is beginning to be noted for its market.

1603 – James I of England and VI of Scotland – Serious outbreak of the Plague

Roger Banne, the Vicar of Leek, has no degree or licence to preach.

1604 – The value of the vicarage is given as £10 per year.

There is a stipendiary priest, named Pott, who holds a licence to preach.

William Adderley conveys Westwood Grange to Francis Trentham of Rocester.

1605 – Gunpowder Plot and the arrest of Guy Fawkes

1607 – The founding of Jamestown, Virginia

The largest timberframed building in the town, Hall House, later the Red Lion Inn, is built on the east side of Market Place by Thomas Jolliffe, who, like earlier members of his family, has prospered in the wool trade. It contained an ornamented plaster ceiling with representation of triumph of death, now preserved at the School of Art.

1608 – East of the Cheddleton road, Ballington Grange Farm existed as Cowhay Farm.

1609 – The Manor of Leek is granted to Sir Christopher Hatton and Sir Francis Needham.

1610 – Sir Christopher Hatton and Sir Francis Needham sell small parts of the manor to John Rothwell of Leek.

1611 – **The authorised version of the Bible published – the King James version**

1612 – The vicar has a house, two little gardens and arable land in Leek Field called Vicars Croft (later Vicars Close) plus a shop at the west end of the Moot Hall, which is let for 6s. 8d., plus the Easter payments of £9 in lieu of tithes.

Sir Christopher Hatton and Sir Francis Needham sell further parts of the manor to Henry Wardle of Leekfrith.

1614 – The licensed preacher is Robert Wattes. He is still there two years later.

1615 – More settlement is taking place on the west side of the town as a result of the piecemeal inclosure of Leek Field.

Timothy Egerton, of Wall Grange in Longsdon, erects a horse mill at Birchall, but Thomas Rudyard forces him to abandon it.

1619 – John Rothwell of Leek dies and gives £1 8s. 0d. a year for four sermons to be preached; the money coming from rent of £10 10s. 0d., charged on land at 'Hellsend', (probably Hillswood End) in Leekfrith and at Horsecroft in Tittesworth, and also to provide weekly dole of 7d. to six poor people in Leek, with the residue going to the vicar for sermons.

1620 – Ball Haye Hall is granted by Sir Ralph Bagnall to Henry Davenport.

1622 – There is a conveyance of a moiety (half) of a burgage.

1623 – Timothy Egerton and his brother Thomas convey Birchall Grange to William Jolliffe of Leek.

John Rothwell, a Leek mercer (a dealer in (usually) textiles of the higher quality) dies. His goods include seven dozen scythes and six hundredweight cwt of bar iron in his "*iron seller*".

1624 – **The Dutch settle in New Amsterdam (now New York)**

1625 – **Charles I**

1626 – Francis Trentham dies and is succeeded by his son, Sir Thomas Trentham, who inherits Westwood Grange.

The Roebuck public house in Derby Street is dated from this year.

1627 – William Jolliffe builds a "large black and white half-timbered building in Market Place". It is later to be the Red Lion.

1628 – The main part of Bone Farm, now Home Farm, is dated 1628, and the cross wing is probably a little earlier.

1628 – Sir Thomas Trentham dies, two years after his father, and his widow, Prudence, goes to live at Westwood.

1629 – The Crown grants Thomas Jodrell of Moorhouse in Leek the right to a threeday fair on 7, 8, and 9 May with a Court of Pie Powder. (A Pie Powder Court is one constituted to deal specifically with disputes at the market and the fair. Speed is of the essence as all parties wish to be away to the next market. It is so called because the parties to the disputes were usually merchants and came to the court with the dust of the market on their feet. The French "pied poudre" means literally "dusty feet".) The Jodrells acquire the right to the market tolls as well. Prudence, the widow of Sir Thomas Trentham, is living at the family's Westwood Grange when she is "*compounded for recusancy*". She conforms soon afterwards and attends the parish church.

1630 – Derby Street is being so called.

There is a settlement on Leek Moor, to the east of the town.

1632 – Randle Ashenhurst, of Ashenhurst in Bradnop, has a horse mill in town

1634 – Church Street is being so called.

The earliest of the existing church registers begins. Church registers earlier than this date did once exist but had been lost by the early 20th century.

1635 – Thomas Rudyard's son, also Thomas, challenges Randle Ashenhurst's right to a mill, claiming that the inhabitants of the manor are obliged to grind their corn at Thomas's mills at Leek and Dieulacres and pay a toll of one sixteenth. That claim is itself challenged in a subsequent inquiry, at least as far as corn bought from outside the manor is concerned. It is also pointed out that the horse mill proved to be especially useful when the manorial mills were put out of action by floods or frosts. The horse mill is probably located in Derby Street.

1636 – The bridge across the River Churnet on the Congleton Road is known as White's Bridge after the family occupying Coneygray House on the Leekfrith side of the river. It is a stone bridge of two small arches, which proves to be inadequate in times of flood.

1637 – Spout Street (later St Edward Street) is being so called.

1638 – Barngates and Beggars Way (later Beggars Lane) are inhabited.

1641 – **Cotton goods first manufactured in Manchester**

Four recusants recorded in the town

1642 – **The Civil War begins**

Sir Christopher Hatton's son, Christopher, Baron Hatton, makes a further sale to William Jolliffe of Leek.

During the Civil War, Leek is largely Parliamentarian. A Royalist force comes into the Leek area in November but is driven away.

A group of inhabitants of the Leek constablewick agree to build a cage or prison.

1643 – February, a band of Moorlanders mount an unsuccessful attack on Stafford. They appeal to the Parliamentary commanders in Cheshire and Derbyshire for assistance but receive only a few men sent to Leek to help with the training. In May, a Parliamentary garrison is established at Leek. Its commander is Lt Col Peter Stepkin. The Moorlanders play a prominent part in the capture of Stafford later in May. In December, Royalist forces under Lord Eythin enter Leek.

Stanley Street

1644 – By March, a Parliamentary Committee is set up in Leek, one of three in Staffordshire; the others being at Stafford and Tamworth. In May, Col John Bowyer of Knypersley is appointed as the governor of Leek.

Elizabeth St Andrew, the widow of William St Andrew of Gotham (Notts) and the daughter of John Wedgwood of Harracles in Longsdon, dies and leaves 6s. 8d. for a sermon every Good Friday. She also leaves rent of 13s. 4d., charged on land in Gayton, for distribution to the poor of Leek on Good Friday.

Francis Trentham dies young and is succeeded by his father's brother, Sir Christopher Trentham.

1645 – February, Col Bowyer takes the Leek garrison to help in the attack on Shrewsbury.

The townships in the Totmonslow Hundred are ordered to send armed watchmen to guard Leek. (A "Hundred" was originally an area of land that supported one hundred families. The name continued for centuries as an administrative district.)

1646 – Sheepmarket and Custard Street (later Stanley Street) are being so called. The name "Custard Street" is derived from "costard", a large apple, and the street is where such apples are sold.

1647 – September, arrangements still being made for quartering troops in the Leek area.

1648 – The Vicar of Leek, Francis Bowyer, signs the Staffordshire Testimony in favour of Presbyterianism. Randle Sillitoe signs the Cheshire Testimony. He is a relative of the Randle Sillitoe who owns land in Derby Street.

1649 – Charles I executed – the Commonwealth is declared

Thomas Jolliffe of Leek, son of William Jolliffe, attends Charles I on the scaffold.

Sir Christopher Trentham dies and is succeeded by his brother William.

By an agreement reached between the inhabitants of Leek and Leekfrith, the rebuilding of White's Bridge on the Congleton Road is begun as a bridge with a single arch but its completion is delayed by the refusal of some of the inhabitants of Leekfrith to contribute towards the cost.

1650 – Cheddleton, Horton and Ipstones have become separate parishes.

1651 – The town constable states that the town has no pillory, cage or other prison but only a pair of stocks. The Court of Quarter Sessions orders a levy on the constablewick to make provision for a cage and a pillory.

1652 – The new Vicar of Leek, Robert Fowler, styles himself "pastor" in the parish register, an indication of his Presbyterian sympathy. George Fox (Founder of "the Society of Friends" – the Quakers) preaches at Caldon.

William Trentham dies and his heir is Francis Trentham's daughter, Elizabeth, a minor.

1653 – Leek is one of the twelve places in Staffordshire which benefit in rotation from a double lecture delivered on the last Friday of each month which has been founded by John Machin of Seabridge in StokeuponTrent, a Presbyterian minister. The lectures are given from 1653 to 1660.

1654 – George Parker of Park Hall in Caverswall is practising law at Leek.

John Machin's friend, Henry Newcome, conducts and witnesses marriages in Leek.

The first Quaker missionary to visit Leek, Richard Hickock, disrupts a service at St Edward's Church and is ejected by the congregation. The first converts included William Davenport of Fould Farm, Leekfrith; Matthew Dale of Rudyard; and Thomas Hammersley of Basford, Cheddleton, each of whom establishes a meeting at his home.

Sheepmarket and Custard Street are being used for specialised trading.

William Fox, the Quaker, visits the Leek Meeting House at the rear of the Old Cock Inn at the bottom of the Market Place.

1655 – Thomas Parker witnesses a marriage in town. He may have been George Parker's elder brother, also a lawyer, or George's second son, another lawyer.

A Quaker convert, William Yardley, of Dairy House, Horton, is imprisoned for speaking out in Leek Church.

1656 – The Market Cross is mentioned as the place where banns are published.

George Parker's soninlaw, Richard Levinge, is a lawyer living in the town.

Richard Hickock, the Quaker missionary, returns to Leek. The Justices of the Peace place armed men outside Quaker meeting places and put into the stocks those who travel to hear him.

Market Cross

Richard Parker, the son of George Parker, a lawyer, is baptised in Leek. He is to become the Attorney General for Ireland, Chief Justice of the Irish Court of Common Pleas, and a baronet.

1656 – Quaker missionary Richard Hickock returns and disputes with the Ranters.

1657 – Elizabeth becomes the wife of Richard Cockayne, later Viscount Cullen.

The banns of Robert Fernyhough of Ipstones, carpenter, and Ellen Smith, are called in the Market Square.

1658 – Quaker missionary Richard Hickock returns again. He confronts a woman who is a member of the "Family of Love".

A surgeon named John Hulme is practising at Leek.

1660 – Baptists and Ranters have become numerous in the Leek area. Quaker missionaries seek to convert them, with some success. Quakers establish meetings in the area.

There are several fairs in Leek, including one on All Souls' Day (2 November).

The road down to the River Churnet, now Broad Street, is known as Spooner's Lane.

Two other Quaker missionaries, Oliver Atherton and Richard Moore, visit Leek.

The graveyard of St Edward's Church has a wall around it.

1661 – **Charles II**

1662 – The 17th-century front of numbers 2 and 4 Church Street are reconstructed in stone and a timber staircase turret and an attic floor are added. The work may well have been carried out for Thomas Parker, lawyer.

The vicar, George Roades, states that the vicarage is "*a large pile of half-timbered building, very old and ruinous*".

1663 – The south porch of the church is repaired, and also the clock.

1664 – Thomas Parker and his father, George Parker, are both lawyers, living in Leek. He is the father of Thomas Parker, later Lord Chancellor and the Earl of Macclesfield.

In a letter to Bishop Hacket the vicar, George Roades draws attention to his labours in "*these barren bogs & heathenish moors*" where he meets almost daily opposition from "*gainsayers*".

With the support of Anthony Rudyard of Dieulacres in Leekfrith, Timothy Edge of Horton Hall and William Jolliffe of Leek, all of them Justices of the Peace, members of church at Leek develop Presbyterian sympathies.

1665 – **The Great Plague**

The church is known to have had a spire.

1666 – **The Great Fire of London**

The Cock public house is on the corner of Market Place and Stockwell Street.

Westwood, the home of Ralph Lees, is assessed for tax on seven hearths. The number assessed for hearth tax is seventy-six in Leek and seventeen in Lowe hamlet. (All governments require taxes. The problem is how to distinguish the rich (who can pay) from the poor (who cannot). This solution seems to have worked quite well, on the basis that the richer a man is, the bigger his house will be, and the more fireplaces he will have. Therefore, count the hearths and the tax collector has a rough-and-ready guide to the wealth of the taxpayer!)

1667 – Thomas Parker, later Lord Chancellor, is born at the house which is now numbers 2 and 4 Church Street, the son of Thomas Parker, lawyer.

An ironmonger named Thomas Brough is living in Leek.

William Fox, the Quaker, visits the Leek Meeting House at the rear of the Old Cock Inn for the second time.

1668 – Leek's first known bookseller, Joseph Needham, has shop premises at the south east corner of the Market Square.

1669 – It is as the bailiff of the town and of the market and as the collector of the market tolls that Thomas's Jodrell's greatnephew, John Jodrell, claims a seat in the north aisle of the parish church, adding that his father, his grandfather and his ancestors had all held the seat by the same right.

William Jolliffe dies. He made £80,000 from the wool trade.

1670 – The silk industry has reached Leek. It will develop steadily in the 18th century, with buttons as the staple product.

The earliest known clockmaker in Leek, Samuel Stretch, a member of a Quaker family, is making lantern clocks. His nephew, Peter Stretch, is also a Leek clockmaker.

A few houses have been built in "Back of the Street" (later Belle Vue Road), on the northwest side of Leek Field.

The present south porch is built at St Edward's Church. The church has at least five bells.

Leek is noted for its excellent ale.

Leek has become one of three most important markets in Staffordshire.

The buildings in Leek are described as being "*but poor and for most part thatched*".

1671 – The market cross is erected at the south end of Market Place by one of the Jolliffe family, probably Thomas.

1672 – There is mention of a little lichgate at St Edward's Church.

The house of Thomas Nabes is licensed for Presbyterian worship. The Presbyterians registered the first place of worship for Nonconformists in the town, following the Declaration of Indulgence that year. (Issued by Charles II and granting religious toleration to all Nonconformists, it is withdrawn the following year as a result of Parliamentary pressure from middle-class members of Parliament.)

John Wood, a silk weaver of Derby Street (ten years later, he is to be described as being a "Button Man"), dies possessing silk worth over £300, "shop goods" worth £100, including ribbons known as galloons, and looms and wheels worth £4 1s. The wheels may have been used for twisting. His goods consist of undyed silk valued at

£179 1s. 0d.; buttons valued at £100; silk at London valued at £18; silk for warfing valued at £6; and more silk valued at £110. He has debts totalling £256 4s. 2d. This is the first clear evidence of silk working in Leek, thus showing that the suggestion that silk working was first brought to Leek by French Protestant refugees after 1685 is erroneous. Thomas Wardle, a leading figure in industry in the 19th century, later stated that the twisting of sewing silks came to Leek from Macclesfield.

1673 – William Hulme, a doctor of physic and surgeon, owns Lower Tittesworth.

1674 – Quaker women's meetings begin. The minutes survive for the years 1709 to 1717.

The north door of St Edward's Church is repaired.

1675 – Stone has become the normal building material. Its use is visible in party walls, as at 47 Derby Street and 13 St Edward Street. Another example of a stone house is 7 Stockwell Street, where despite an 18thcentury brick façade the stone gable is visible.

By will, John Stoddard of Thorneyleigh Green Farm in Leekfrith leaves £1 year for a sermon to be preached on the third Wednesday in April, June and September. (It has been changed to May, July and September by 1726.)

The town has become noted for its market, with a considerable trade in cattle, sheep, oats and provisions. The market is ranked as the third most important in the county, after Uttoxeter and Wolverhampton. Wednesday is the market day.

The Barnfields farm, east of the Newcastle road, exists.

William Yardley preaches at a conventicle (an illegal religious meeting, held secretly) held at the house of Sarah Sleigh and Hannah Hay in Leek. They are arrested and he is fined £20 and the women £10 each.

The Hollinshead family, the Ashenhursts' successors at Ashenhurst, have a horse mill in Derby Street. It remains there for nearly fifty years.

By the late 17th century, Greystones in Stockwell Street has been built.

Greystones

Alms houses

1676 – Elizabeth Ashe, the daughter of William Jolliffe of Leek, and the widow of Edward Ashe, a London draper, has eight almshouses built at the corner of Broad Street and Compton. The occupants are to be widows or spinsters aged at least sixty, or in some way disabled, and resident in the parish. Each resident is to receive a weekly dole of 1s. 8d. from the vicar on Sunday, and every two years is to have a new gown of violet cloth, embroidered with the initials EA. As an endowment she gives rent of £40 charged on land at Mixon, in Onecote. She personally chooses the first almswomen and instructs that, after her death, one is to be chosen by her brother Thomas Jolliffe and his heirs, another by her son William Ashe and his heirs, and the other six by Jolliffe and Ashe jointly with the vicar, the churchwardens and the Overseers of the Poor of the Leek parish. Of those six, three are to come from the rural quarters of the parish, Bradnop, Endon and Leekfrith.

1677 – The rectory forms part of the Rudyard Hall estate. The library for the Anglican clergy of Leek originates in a bequest by Margaret Shallcross, the daughter of Thomas Rudyard and the widow of Edmund Shallcross, the rector of Stockport, who leaves her husband's books to the vicars of Leek. She also gives a rent charge of 20s. to repair and augment the collection.

One of St Edward's Church's five bells is recast at Nottingham.

1678 – Elizabeth Ashe's aunt Anne, the wife of Sir John Dethick, Lord Mayor of London, gives £100, the interest on which is to be spent on coal for the poor of Leek.

1680 – Members of the Society of Friends in the Leek area have joined together to form a monthly meeting. The Presbyterians are meeting in Derby Street.

The Easter payments are assessed at a rate of 1s. for a house with twenty acres or more attached and 9d. for a house of lesser status occupied by a married man, and 7d. for one occupied by an unmarried or widowed person; plus 2d. for every boarder or child. Heaton, Rushton James and Rushton Spencer are exempt from the Easter payments.

The vicar also received a modus (a fixed payment instead of the collection of tithes, which were becoming difficult to collect) of 5s. 6d. year for tithe of hay in Endon.

The poor people of area are *"employed much in making of buttons"*.

Robert Plot notes that at Leek *"they build chiefly with a redish sort of stone"* quarried locally.

In the Millstone Grit of the Leek area there are outcrops of sandstone known as crowstones with a high silica content. Although not suitable for building, they are quarried for road metal and for walling stone.

The steep descent down from the town, now known as Mill Street, is known as *"the hollow lane"*.

Leek and Lowe is a township which forms one of the quarters of Leek parish, and has its own churchwarden and its own Overseer of the Poor. Leek and Lowe, Heaton, Leekfrith, Rushton Spencer and Tittesworth are part of the Leek constablewick.

The day of 17 July is designated as a Fair Day.

Over 40 acres of common waste on the north side of the Town Field, consisting of Woodcroft Heath, Westwood Heath and land at Nab Hill and the Back of the Street (later Belle Vue Road), pass to the freeholders of Leek and Lowe township. The income from rents charged for pasturing horses there and rents from houses built at Back of Street is used for the repair of the highways and other public purposes.

Henry Davenport of Ball Haye Hall dies, aged ninety-three.

1682 – Jonathan Wood, son of John Wood, is a silk weaver living in Leek.

1683 – Wild boars become extinct in Britain

Land in Derby Street is owned by Randle Sillitoe, a feltmaker who is probably a relative of the Randle Sillitoe who signed the Cheshire Testimony in favour of Presbyterianism in 1648. This land may have been the site of two cottages which are apparently rented in 1695 by Josiah Hargrave (or Hargreaves), who is later recorded as being the Presbyterian minister in Leek.

Congregationalists meet in the loft of a stable off Derby Street (probably at the back the Black's Head, but could be the site of the present Trinity Church).

1684 – The arched and pinnacled stone gateway to St Edward's Church on the south side is built.

1685 – James II – French Huguenots arrive in England

1688 – By will, Joan Armett of Thorneyleigh Hall Farm, Leekfrith, leaves money for charitable purposes; rent of £2 13s. 4d. being charged on land in Leekfrith to be distributed on Christmas Eve to the poor of Leek town, with preference being given to those living in Mill Street.

Mention is made of Leek's *"new market day"*.

1689 – William and Mary

William Watson, a grocer, leaves to the poor of Leek income from land near Barngates, with a tithe of corn from the land. Among his goods at his death are "apothecary ware" and tobacco.

1690 – Stockwood Street is in existence (later renamed Stockwell Street).

John Hulme leaves to the poor of Leek town and parish the rent from half of the first crop from four days' mowing of a meadow called Leadbetters (later Poor's) meadow; the funds to be distributed at Christmas.

At the church, communion services are being held on Palm Sunday, Good Friday, Easter Sunday, Low Sunday, Whit Sunday, Trinity Sunday, the Sunday before and after Michaelmas, the last Sunday in December and the first Sunday in January. There is not a communion service held on every Sunday.

Gervase Gent, a Quaker, dies. He is an apothecary and he owns property in America. Leek Friends have connections with Quaker settlements in America. It is the property that he leaves which indicate his trade and suggests that he is an apothecary and a barber/surgeon. They include drugs and allied equipment, a urinal, clyster pipes, razors and "some instruments of chirurgery".

The Presbyterians' meetings are held outside town.

William Hulme, a minister of Newton Solney (Derbyshire), leaves interest on £26 13s. 4d. to the poor of Leek town and parish. The capital is given to a relative, Robert Hulme, whose son, John Hulme (dies 1690) of Thorncliffe secures the charity by his will.

The timberframed vicarage house is in a ruinous state.

1692 – Matthew Stubbs dies. He combined the button trade with farming, and besides cloth, his stock contains a large quantity of buttons, including thread buttons, hair buttons and braid buttons.

1693 – William Hulme, a doctor of physic and surgeon, dies.

The Green Dragon tavern is in existence.

Thomas Jolliffe dies. He is succeeded by his sons John, of Botham Hall in Cheddleton, and Benjamin, of Cofton Hackett, Worcestershire. By his will, he gives £4 a year for a lecture to be delivered on the first Wednesday of every month.

1694 – John Jolliffe of Botham Hall, Cheddleton, dies.

Land for a Meeting House at Overton Bank is acquired from the daughters of Gervase Gent, a Quaker.

1695 – Bank of England founded

A house is registered for Presbyterian worship at Dunwood, in Longsdon.

The parishioners rebuild part of the vicarage when Thomas Walthall becomes vicar.

John Horsley, a Leek lawyer, dies. He is probably a member of a Bradnop family of that name.

Two cottages in Derby Street are rented by Josiah Hargrave (Hargreaves?), later recorded as Presbyterian minister in Leek.

The Quaker meeting house opens.

William Mills, a lawyer, dies.

A lichgate, a turn gate and a new gate on the north side of St Edward's Church are mentioned.

1696 – The present building consisting of eight almshouses at the corner of Broad Street and Compton carries a plaque with this date on it.

John Jodrell dies and his son William succeeds him

1697 – William Trafford dies. When interrogated by Parliamentary troops during the Civil War he passed himself off as a simpleton by continuing to thresh corn, saying only "*Now thus*". This phrase, and a picture of a man threshing corn, is engraved on his tombstone.

Following a decision by the Society of Friends that there should be a Quaker schoolmaster in each county, the Staffordshire quarterly meeting decides to establish a school at Leek, with the master paid £15 year. They set up a boys' boarding school at Leek, which lasts about 50 years.

William Grosvenor of Leek is licensed to practise as physician and surgeon, his certificate of fitness being signed by the Vicar of Leek; by Thomas Beckett, a surgeon; and by Benjamin Endon, a physician, probably of Dunwood House Farm in Longsdon.

1698 – Three yews are planted in the churchyard of St Edward's Church.

A hostelry known as the Red Lion is in existence, but the site is not known.

It is stated that the churchyard has always belonged to the vicar.

Elizabeth Ashe dies. Thomas Jolliffe and William Ashe and their heirs seem not to have exercised their right to nominate the residents at the almshouses.

Thomas Walthall becomes the vicar and the vicarage is rebuilt in part.

1699 – Presbyterian worship takes place in a house registered at Westwood.

THE EIGHTEENTH CENTURY

1700 – **The population of England and Scotland is about 7.5 million**

William Jodrell mortgages the market and fair tolls to John Sutton and William Grosvenor, a Leek physician.

At a quarterly meeting of the Society of Friends, the schoolmaster, Joseph Davison, is allowed to admit the sons of nonQuakers. The fees are used, together with a grant from the quarterly meeting, to set up a fund to provide scholarships for the sons of poor Quakers.

A church school is held in the north aisle of the parish church. It included boys aged fourteen and fifteen.

The highest number of communicants in the Church is 62 on Easter Sunday, with 40 on Palm Sunday and 35 on Good Friday. The lowest is sixteen on Whit Sunday.

1701 – Joseph Davison, the Quaker schoolmaster, is imprisoned for teaching without a licence. The school survives.

Josiah Hargrave, who lives at Westwood, is left £20 by Roger Morrice. He has been ejected as vicar of Duffield (Derbyshire) in 1662. The bequest is conditional on Hargrave's continuing to preach at Westwood, or at any other place "in the Moorlands" for at least two years after Morrice's death.

The church books are being kept in a press in the vicarage house.

The Easter payment is fixed at one shilling for land worth £20 or more.

1702 –   Queen Anne

Samuel Stretch, a clockmaker, emigrates with his family to Philadelphia. He will make longcase clocks there.

1704 –   The gallery in St Edward's Church, described as "*the new gallery*", is being repaired. It may have been the west gallery.

1705 –   John Condliffe of Leek is described as a barber/surgeon.

William Grosvenor is described as an apothecary.

Pickwood Farm, to the southeast of the town, exists.

The glebe is worth £6 a year. The Easter payments should have been worth nearly £30 a year, but because of the poverty of the people and the cost and trouble of collecting it in so large a parish, its actual value is £20. Surplice fees could amount to nearly £15. The vicar complained that Dissenters, and especially Quakers, "*do by their obstinacy draw the vicar into many tedious and expensive suits for the recovery of his just rights*", with the result that the value of the vicarage is considerably reduced.

Thomas Parker of Leek is made Lord Chief Justice (some accounts state this to be in 1710).

Thomas Parker

1706 – An "*abundance of Presbyterians & Quakers & some Anabaptists*" are noted in Leek parish.

1707 – The Quakers plan to send two Leek children, who are staying at John Stretch's home in Leek, to Pennsylvania.

An apothecary named William Thorpe dies.

William Condlyffe is born at Upper Hulme. He will later become a solicitor.

1708 – It is stated that the vicars of Leek have always been allowed 12d. for every mile which they have to travel within the parish to baptise a child away from the church.

Horse races are being held in October, probably connected with the wake (public holiday).

The Quaker Meeting House has a gallery.

Freeholders attempt an action against the encroachments on the Leek Moor, east of the town.

1709 – The vicar, Thomas Walthall, states that he reads prayers every morning.

Death of William Jolliffe. West Farm passes to his daughter Lucy, the wife of William Vane.

Quaker Meeting House

1710 – The bridge at Wallbridge consists of a wooden horse bridge with a dangerous ford adjoining it. Travellers suffer both losses and delays from frequent flooding of the river.

1711 – A catalogue of books in the vicarage is compiled by the vicar, James Osbourne. He lists 44 folio volumes, 67 quarto, 17 octavo and 41 bound in leather.

At the Leek monthly meeting of the Quakers, Joseph Davison, the schoolmaster, indicates his willingness to be left "*to his liberty for some consideration, yet willing upon our request to serve us*". His salary is increased by £3 year.

The income from the common land on the north of town (Belle Vue area) amounts to £2 15s. 6d.

1712 – John Oakes, a tobacconist, dies. He is succeeded by Thomas Oakes of Leek.

A petition from 83 inhabitants of Totmonslow Hundred is presented to the Court of Quarter Sessions which grants £60 to rebuild the bridge at Wallbridge in stone for carts and carriages.

William Grosvenor is described as a physician.

A separate monthly Quaker meeting is being held alternately at Whitehough and Bottom House. These amalgamate with the Leek meeting.

1713 – Rebecca, the wife of Sir Samuel Moyer, establishes an English school at Leek, the birthplace of her father: the John Jolliffe school for fifty poor children of Leek and Cheddleton. Each child is given three years' tuition. A schoolmaster is appointed and he is instructed to pay strict attention to his pupils' morals and to ensure that they attend church every Sunday and Holy Day. He is paid £20 a year. Rebecca undertakes to provide new books every three years and to buy bibles as leaving presents for the children.

George Jackson is appointed as the vicar.

George Roades, rector of Blithfield and the son of George Roades, the vicar of Leek 1662–95, dies and leaves tithe corn from several plots of land in Leek to the vicar for ever. His will also provides for the establishment of an English school at Leek for poor children aged six to ten.

1714 – George I

By will, James Rudyard of Dieulacres Abbey leaves rent of £2 15s. charged on land in Leekfrith to endow a bread dole. One-penny loaves are to be distributed to twelve poor people at St Edward's Church every Sunday after the evening service and on Christmas Day, Good Friday and Ascension Day. Beneficiaries unable to come to church because of ill health are to be sent a loaf. He also charges his estate with an annual payment of £2 to the vicar.

The rest of the vicarage is rebuilt and enlarged, with the parishioners contributing £100. The summerhouse in the garden, with a stable under it, is built, or rebuilt, at the same time.

1715 – The First Jacobite Rebellion

Several people in Leek declare for the Pretender.

A dancing master is teaching in Leek.

Building stone is being dug in the common land known as Back of Street (later Belle Vue Road).

The Presbyterians have a Meeting House in Derby Street. It is first recorded when it is damaged by rioters. It stood on the west side of the Roebuck Inn.

Thomas Oakes is described as a tobacconist.

1716 – Thomas Parker is created Baron Parker of Macclesfield.

Josiah Hargrave is still living at Westwood. He is responsible for the Presbyterian Meeting House in Derby Street.

James Brindley is born at Wormhill, Derbyshire.

1717 – The Grand Masonic Lodge established in England

William Mills (later Sheriff of Staffordshire) is born at the house later known as Foxlowe.

Thomas Mills born.

Lady Moyer gives in trust for the school a ninety-year annuity of £25 and amplifies her plan for the school. The master is to be a layman. He is to receive £20 a year for teaching fifty children to read and write. Both he and the children are to be chosen by the Board of Governors, including the vicar and the churchwardens. The children are to be admitted at the age of six and are to remain at school until they are able to read and write. The vicar is to be paid £1 a year for catechising them once a fortnight. The sum of £4 a year is to be spent on bibles, primers and catechisms. In addition, every Sunday after the sermon, the children are to be allowed to sing hymns learnt at school.

The congregation at the Presbyterian Meeting House in Derby Street numbers 250 "*hearers*".

1718 – Thomas Oakes, hitherto a tobacconist, is described as a grocer.

Thomas Parker is created Lord Chancellor.

By will, William Dudley of Fields in Horton, and formerly of Lyme House in Longsdon, leaves 6s. 8d. for a sermon to be preached on 29 May, the anniversary of Charles II's restoration.

1719 – A pulpit with a reading desk and a sounding board is installed in the church.

The private schools in the town seem to have catered primarily for children of townspeople. They tended to be small schools and shortlived. A girls' school is opened by Margaret Brindley, later Margaret Lucas.

1720 – The girls' school opened by Margaret Brindley closes amid family quarrels when she becomes a Quaker.

The grammar school opens but remains small and poor. Boys from the Leek area who are intended for the universities continue to be sent to school elsewhere.

William Vane is created Viscount Vane (d. 1734).

Westwood Farm is the property of William Jolliffe of Caverswall Castle.

Itinerant singing masters visit the town.

A group of twenty-two townsmen, aware of the need for a grammar school, successfully petition the Bishop to license as a grammar school master one Thomas Bourne, who settles in Leek in January.

A chapel is built at Endon.

Elizabeth, the daughter of Thomas Parker (Lord Chancellor), marries William Heathote, MP for Buckingham.

1721 – Leek joins with several Cheshire towns in successfully petitioning on behalf of all those employed in the manufacture of "*needlewrought buttons*" for the passing of an Act banning the wearing of cloth buttons and buttonholes.

Thomas Parker is created Earl of Macclesfield.

The bells of St Edward's Church are recast as a peal of six by Abraham Rudhall of Gloucester.

As an experiment for the summer months, it is agreed to hold two Quaker meetings for worship at Leek on Sundays: one at 10.30 a.m. for both "country" and "town" members and another at 3 p.m. for "town" members.

1722 – William Mills junior is practising law.

Both sets of tolls (market and fair) are conveyed to William Grosvenor.

Eli Robinson is practising as an apothecary in Leek. Henry Fogg, the son of a Stone butcher, is apprenticed to him.

1723 – Thomas Parker buys the manor of Leek, at his second attempt, and builds the grammar school on Clerk Bank. It has a symmetrical front of ashlar (squared stone used in building or in a facing wall).

William Condlyffe is articled to Richard Goodwin.

Benjamin Watson of Leek is described as barber/surgeon.

The capital left by Anne Dethick (see 1678) is used, together with £100 left for the poor of Leek town by Thomas Jolliffe (d.1693) and £10 similarly left by Mrs Haywood of Macclesfield to buy 22½ acres at Oulton, in Rushton Spencer. The almswomen are entitled to 10/21 parts of the rent from the land, with the remainder being for the poor of Leek town.

William Grosvenor is described as a physician.

The burial mound described as Cock Lowe, or the Great Lowe, is still standing at the southwest of the town between Waterloo Road and Spring Gardens.

1724 – No. 62 St Edward Street is built with an ashlar front.

Lady Moyer's will is proved. It confirms the provisions made for the English School in Leek and asks that the annuity should be used to buy land to endow the school. That request is not carried out. She also leaves a copy of Isaac Barrow's *Sermons* and one volume of John Foxe's *Book of Martyrs* to be kept chained in the church.

St Edward Street

The town has a fire engine, given by the Earl of Macclesfield, after his purchase of the manor. It is maintained by the churchwardens.

1725 – Thomas Parker (Lord Chancellor) is impeached, convicted of corruption, removed from office and fined £30,000.

William Badnall has dye-houses by the River Churnet in Abbey Green Road at its junction with Mill Street.

The Quaker Meeting House in Leek is the largest in Staffordshire. Its contribution to national funds is twice that of Stafford's.

In St Edward's Church, a gallery for "*the charity children*" is erected.

Thomas Loxdale is appointed the Vicar of Leek. He stays until 1735.

James Brindley, aged ten, and his family move to a farm at Lowe Hill.

1727 – George II

Worcestershire and mountain elms are planted on the north side of St Edward's Church.

William Fallowfield of Leek obtains a patent for making iron with peat. He delays putting it into operation *"because of a mighty bustle"* by the Wolverhampton ironmaster William Wood, who is attempting to smelt iron with pit coal at Chelsea.

In the almshouses that have been built at the corner of Broad Street and Compton, there has still has been no almswoman from Endon and only one from Bradnop. It is agreed that all almswomen should be chosen by the vicar together with the churchwardens and the overseers, who also agree to put the names of the quarters (parts of the parish) over the doors of houses assigned to them. The houses still bear those names and the names "Jolliffe", "Ash" and (in three instances) "Leek". The almshouses form an Lshaped building, with six dwellings facing Broad Street and two Compton. Originally they are singlestorey.

1728 – The Cock, on the corner of Market Place and Stockwell Street, is sold by the Mellor family to John Toft of Haregate in Tittesworth.

Joseph Myott of Church Street is described as a silk weaver.

Westwood Farm, occupied by Caleb Morrice, consists of 403 acres. The house is in a bad state of repair. There is also a fourteen-acre farm and a thirteen-acre *"Cunney Greave"* or rabbit warren.

Robert Key, a member of a local Quaker family, practises as a physician in Leek, having studied at Leiden.

Thomas Jodrell of Endon dies. He leaves one third of the interest on £200 for the poor of Leek. Eli Robinson is described as a surgeon and apothecary when he attends him on his deathbed.

1729 – Joseph Jackson occupies a shed (locally known as shade) for twisting mohair, at Spout Gate at the south end of Spout Street (later St Edward Street).

1730 – William Condlyffe practises law in Leek.

1731 – William Fallowfield has a furnace near Leek.

1732 – The Quaker School is described as a grammar school where boys are boarded and taught writing and accounts.

Thomas Parker, former Lord Chancellor, dies, aged 66.

Leek joins with Manchester, Macclesfield and Stockport in petitioning against the renewal of John Lombe's patent for his silk-throwing mill in Derby. The petitioners include the manufacturers of silk and mohair yarn and twisters and twiners of mohair, cotton, worsted, and probably linen thread.

Samuel Toft dies. He was a Quaker button merchant of Leek and has stock worth £634 6s. *"in shops at Salop and Hereford"*. He also has cattle and goods at Pickwood Farm worth £29.

Shortly before her death, Anne Jolliffe, the daughter of Thomas, Lord Crew, and widow of John Jolliffe of Cheddleton, gives the interest on £250 to be shared by the curate of Cheddleton (£4 a year), twelve poor widows of Cheddleton (£1 4s. 0d a year) and the poor widows of Leek (the remainder). The money is used to buy land at Compton and near Cornhill Cross.

1733 – *The London Magazine* publishes a poem by 'H. C.' lauding Thomas Bourne's skill as a teacher of classics.

Joseph Grundy, of Leek, dies. He is described as being a tobacconist.

James Brindley is apprenticed to wheelwrights at Sutton, Macclesfield.

William Heathcote, the son-in-law of Thomas Parker (ex-Lord Chancellor), is created a baronet.

1734 – Joseph Myott of Church Street has a twisting alley next to his house. It seems that the twisting of mohair, rather than silk, predominated in Leek for much of the 18th century.

The silkmen of Leek unite with those of Macclesfield and the Lancashire towns in a campaign against John Lombe's water-powered twisting process.

William Badnall (d. 1760) of Mill Street works as a dyer.

1735 – The Quaker meeting comprises 125 adults and children, at least a third of whom live outside the town.

William Fallowfield's furnace is still working in Leek.

Joseph Grosvenor is supplying medicines.

1736 – The Quaker Library consists of some 200 books.

William Badnall is described as a mohair dyer.

Randle Maddock, a prolific clockmaker, is working in Stockwell Street.

1737 – Ribbons are among the stock of Mary Davenport, Leek chapwoman (itinerant pedlar), at her death. They were probably made locally.

The last four vicars have added another 34 volumes to the list of books at the church. Thomas Loxdale, who added twenty of them, stated that the library has been much diminished before coming into his hands and that less of the income has been spent on books than might have been expected.

1738 – A house at Barngates is described as a messuage or burgage.

William Mills, a lawyer, has been joined by his son Thomas.

1739 – A new font is installed in the church. The old one may have been placed outside the building.

John Naylor of Leek dies. He has directed his executors to secure an annuity of £50 for the poor of Leek town. He also leaves £5 to provide a sermon on his birthday, 12 October.

It is stated that the west gallery in St Edward's Church has been in existence beyond living memory. A new west gallery is built this year, extending over the un-aisled part of the nave.

1740 – George Anson sets out on voyage around the world

John Finney dies. He is described as a cheese factor, but the house and shop contained flax, hemp, jersey, woollen and linen cloth, and woollen and worsted yarn, plus hose for adults and children, caps and a stocking frame.

The Cock, on the corner of Market Place and Stockwell Street, has eighteen rooms with one or more beds.

Joseph Grosvenor practises as a lawyer in Cheadle.

1741 – John Naylor's charity is established.

By will, William Grosvenor leaves interest on £20 to be distributed on St Thomas's Day (21 December) to the poor householders of Leek town.

1742 – First performance of Handel's *Messiah*

Thomas Fernyhough is the town crier at the time of his death.

James Brindley sets up as a millwright in Mill Street.

Thomas Mills, a lawyer, of Leek, acquires the manor of Barlaston by marriage.

A Leek ironmonger named James Hall dies.

1743 – Richard Ferne's dye-house is newly erected in Abbey Green Road. It also has "*poles for drying linen yarn*" by the brook.

A Leek watchmaker named Richard Steen dies.

Richard Ferne is described as a thread merchant.

1744 – The Green Dragon inn at Leek is the meeting place of the Court Leet (a Court of Record presided over by the Lord of the Manor or his Steward).

John Pott of Leek is trading as a tobacconist.

1745 – The Second Jacobite Rebellion

Prince Charles Edward and his army pass through Leek on their way to Derby. Bonnie Prince Charlie wants to stay in the vicarage "but vicar's wife would not suffer him to *molliter manus imosuit*"– she simply pushed him out. On 3 December, a Scottish detachment, under Lord George Murray, passes through Leek, on its way to Ashbourne. The main force with the prince arrives in Leek later the same day and takes up quarters there. The prince stayed at the house, on the site of Foxlowe, of William Mills, a lawyer. The Quaker Meeting House is broken into and used as a stable. There is no evidence of Jacobite sympathisers. Troops begin to leave Leek for Ashbourne and Derby in the small hours of 4 December. Some remain and try to seize the horses of people coming to the market. Two soldiers are arrested and sent to Stafford gaol. The prince, retreating from Derby, is back in Leek on 7 December. The vanguard of his army goes on to Macclesfield and the rest follow the next day. The houses of the principal inhabitants of Leek are "*totally stripped and plundered*", apparently in revenge for the arrest of the two horse thieves. Mrs Daintry dies on 15 December after the Scots "*put the town and country all into a fright*". The Duke of Cumberland passes through Leek with his pursuing force on 10 December and is entertained in Market Place.

Randle Maddock, the clockmaker in Stockwell Street, is still living in Leek at his death.

1746 – Henry Fogg is described as an apothecary and surgeon. He has numerous clients in the Leek area and beyond.

1747 – Samuel Grosvenor, a Leek grocer, has tobacco and spices in stock when he dies.

No 64 St Edward Street has rainwater hoppers of this date, plus a brick front; in contrast to number 62, which is dated 1724.

Joseph Davison, the Quaker schoolmaster, dies a prosperous man; but the school apparently dies with him.

1748 – Horse races are held in Leek in October.

1749 – A shade (workplace) is newly erected behind the Buffalo's Head public house, which is the inn at the south end of Market Place. It is variously known as The Buffalo's Head and The Bull's Head.

William Mills, a lawyer, dies. By will he leaves interest on £100. After payments of 20s. to the vicar of Leek for a charity sermon on his birthday (20 November) and 5s. to the parish clerk the balance is for distribution of bread on Sundays to poor widows of Leek and Lowe and of Leekfrith.

1750 – The Mills family practise law at Leek. They may have taken over George Parker's practice. They act for the Earls of Macclesfield, and are the town's leading lawyers.

Richard Wilkes, a Staffordshire antiquary, notes Leek's *"great trade of making buttons for men's clothes of hair, mohair, silk thread etc. ... Many hundreds of poor people are employed in this manufacture, get good livelihood, and bring great riches to gentlemen that procure materials to set them to work and patterns to please the wearer."*

The town has been largely rebuilt, with brick replacing stone. By the middle of the century red brick has become the fashionable material for frontages.

Leek Friends (Quakers) seem to have been tolerated but those who married outside the society are disowned.

Fountain Street takes its name from a reservoir at its eastern end.

The town is supplied with water piped from two reservoirs on Leek Moor.

Buckets are provided for fire-fighting and kept at St Edward's Church. They are repaired by the churchwardens of Leek parish.

Leek has seven fairs per year, on the Wednesday before 2 February; the Wednesday in Easter week; 7 May; the Wednesday after Whitsun; 22 June; 17 July; and 2 November. All the fixed dates moved on eleven days with the change of calendar in 1752.

After the death of Henry Fogg, the contents of his shop and his medical books are bought by Hugh Wishaw.

John Davenport is articled to Thomas Gent.

Leading Quakers in the town include Joshua Toft of Haregate Hall, button merchant, and his brother, John, a silk weaver. Both men are also ministers.

1751 – Thomas Bourne, the master, is teaching fifty children the catechism and taking them regularly to church.

There are two services on a Sunday, at 10 a.m. and 2 p.m. There are prayers on Wednesday, Friday and Saturday and on all Holy Days. Children are catechised on Saturday evening during Lent. Communion is administered on the first Sunday in the month and on Christmas Day, Good Friday, Easter Sunday and the Sunday before or after Easter, Whit Sunday and Trinity Sunday. The number of communicants at Easter and Whitsun is nearly 100 and at other times about sixty.

It is estimated that thirty or forty attend the Presbyterian Meeting House in Derby Street. Meetings are held at noon on Sundays and Thursdays.

Hall House in the Market Place becomes the Red Lion Inn.

The Vicar of Leek notes that out of 1,050 families in the parish there are twenty Quakers and sixteen Presbyterians. There are also one or two "*reputed*" Anabaptists. Some thirty or forty people attend the Quaker meeting and a similar number the Presbyterian meeting. This compares with about sixty who attend the monthly Anglican communion service at the parish church.

1752 – Great Britain adopts the Gregorian calendar

William Challinor is born.

James Brindley's watermill in Mill Street opens as a corn mill, after being rebuilt by him.

Thomas Mills junior is born. He becomes a lawyer.

A Quaker button merchant, Joshua Strangman, marries Joshua Toft's niece, Ann Toft. They lived at No. 62 St Edward Street.

1754 – Joseph Condlyffe born, son of William.

Richard Ferne is described as being a threadmaker.

Cornelius Bowman of Pennsylvania visits Leek, where his family are Quakers.

Thomas Mills, a lawyer, is appointed Sheriff of Staffordshire and appoints Thomas Gent his undersheriff.

1755 – The church has a spire.

By will, Thomas Birtles, a Leek button merchant, leaves the interest on £100 to be distributed on St Thomas's Day to poor householders of Leek town.

A Methodist Society of twenty-four members is formed in Leek.

1756 – The Golden Lion probably exists, for a house on this site is sold to a tenant, William Allen, who is described as an "innholder".

Joseph Grosvenor's son, Joshua, is described as being a Leek apothecary.

1757 – A gardener named William Hyde lives in Leek.

William Condlyffe builds a house in Derby Street which remains the family home.

1758 – William Badnall buys the bankrupt Richard Ferne's linenthread works on the opposite side of Abbey Green Road, which includes a dye-house by Ball Haye Brook.

The custom of choosing a Mock Mayor for the town exists, for the officeholder that year is John Sneyd of Bishton, in Colwich.

William Clowes is a Leek schoolmaster.

1759 – William, Viscount Vane, son of William and Lucy Vane, sells the reversion of the "*manor or lordship of Westwood and the farm or grange called Westwood*" to Mary, Countess of Stamford.

The Mock Mayor for the town announces that he will hold a feast at the Cock Inn in January. The occasion is probably identifiable with the annual Venison Feast.

John Davenport is in practice on his own account.

1760   Josiah Wedgwood founds a pottery works at Etruria

The Leek/Buxton road leaves the town along Mill Street. It then runs via Abbey Green and Upper Hulme, and through Quarnford, in Alstonefield, via Flash, to Wallnook, Hartington, and on to Buxton.

The churchwardens try to stop "*the lads*" playing football in the churchyard, especially on Sundays.

A surgeon named Isaac Cope lives in Sheepmarket.

There is a well in Mill Street, west of the junction with Abbey Green Road.

The Mayor of Coventry states that he has sent materials to Leek as well as to Congleton to be made up into ribbons.

Numbers 10, 23 and 25 Derby Street are built.

1761 –   The Bridgewater Canal is finished

Robert Key, a physician, dies at Leek having practised in London. The family are Quakers and included several button merchants.

1762 – Communications are much improved with five main roads into town being "*turnpiked*". The first road to be turnpiked is the Cheddleton road, followed by the road to Macclesfield via Rudyard. A tollhouse is built on the Cheddleton road near to Sheephouse Farm. The road through Leek between Ashbourne and Congleton is turnpiked.

A gardener named Matthew Washington lives in Spout Street.

1763 – Quaker women's meetings are still being held, but irregularly.

The trustees order a gate or chain to be placed at Lowe Hill to prevent unauthorised use of the toll road.

1764 –   American colonies begin to be taxed

Joshua Grosvenor is practising as a surgeon in Leek.

The lane down to Brook Street is called Blackmoreshead Lane (now Pickwood Road).

A turnpike gate is erected at Rudyard.

Joseph Myott is twisting mohair in a shade situated behind the Buffalo's Head inn at the south end of the Market Place.

1765 – A ban is imposed on the import of silk goods. This, plus the improvement of communications, encourages the development of the Leek silk industry.

The road between Newcastle and Hassop via Leek and Longnor is turnpiked with a branch road to Buxton. The stretch northeast from Leek seems to have been largely a new road.

William Clowes, a Leek schoolmaster, is renting part of Barnfield Farm and using it as a schoolhouse.

Thomas Jolliffe's trustees convey Great Birchall Farm, with the nearby Sheephouse Farm and Barnfield Farm, to his nephews Michael, Benjamin, and Francis Biddulph.

The Leek to Buxton road is laid out under the Turnpike Act of 1765.

James Brindley marries Anne Henshall.

A tollhouse is built at Lowe Hill.

Rebecca Lowe, a relative of Thomas Jolliffe, leaves £400 for the almswomen. It is invested in stock.

William Grosvenor, a physician, dies aged 101.

Workhouse

There is mention of a seat called Jodrell's Chapel in the church.

The George Inn is built on the corner of Spout Street and Church Street.

1766 – There is a bowling green in Stockwell Street.

The Biddulphs sell Great Birchall Farm to Harry Lankford of Hurdsfield in Prestbury.

The trustees order a gate and chain to be placed at the east end of Stockwell Street in Leek pending the building of a tollhouse.

1767 – The trustees of the Sandon to Bullock Smithy road announce that the road is completely finished and that it has "*genteel accommodations, good chaises, able horses, and careful drivers*" available at Leek as well as elsewhere. It is also claimed that the road is the shortest route from London to Manchester.

Two ribbon weavers are the only papists in the Leek Parish.

1768 – The workhouse for the Leek and Lowe township is completed in Spout Lane, which is then renamed Workhouse Street (now Brook Street).

1769 – Stone from Edgeend Farm in Tittesworth is being used for road work.

1770 – The croft on which the Quaker Meeting House stands is converted into a garden and a new stable block for use of the Friends who attend the meetings from a distance. The buildings also included a "*house of ease*" (a lavatory). Land on the north side of the meeting house is used for burials.

William Clowes, a schoolmaster, is buried at Leek. He may be the son, or the father, of William Clowes, the Leek schoolmaster who dies in 1774.

The Quaker Cornelius Bowman of Pennsylvania has remained in England (see 1754) and is still associated with the Leek meetings.

1771 – Thomas Bourne, the schoolmaster, dies. The school has no endowment. The Earl of Macclesfield appoints Bourne's successors and remains the owner of the building., the master paying a peppercorn rent and being responsible for its upkeep. For many years his only income apart from fees has come from the charity of George Roades. Eventually enough money is received to buy £323 stock, the income from which is used to pay the master of the grammar school to teach poor children to read.

1772 – An itinerant female minister, Frances Dodshon, is a member of the Leek Quaker meeting.

The tollhouse in Leek is replaced by one at Mile Tree on Leek Moor. It still survives as a private house.

Roman coins forming part of a hoard are found two miles south of the town. It is said that they bore the inscription of the Gallic Emperor Victorinus (269–71).

The organ gallery in St Edward's Church is erected when an organ is installed in the church. The organ is made by Glyn and Parker of Manchester.

James Brindley surveys the route of the Caldon Canal around Ipstones. Caught in a storm, he catches a chill and dies on 27 September, aged 56.

Methodist Preaching is taking place at Nab Hill, but there is no regular meeting place when John Wesley visits the town on 23 March.

1773   Boston Tea Party

Harry Lankford is declared bankrupt.

The first mention is made of the Roebuck public house.

The shade behind the Buffalo's Head is used for stretching and drying mohair by Messrs Phillips and Ford, button merchants.

The Trent and Mersey Canal Company plans a branch canal to Leek from Etruria.

1774 – John Wesley visits Leek again, on 24 July. Joshua Strangman entertains him at 62 St Edward Street.

A room behind the Blackamoor's Head inn in Derby Street is being used by Methodists.

William Clowes, the Leek schoolmaster, dies.

William Condlyffe's elder son John works for him.

Harry Lankford's assignees sell three farms to Allwood Wilkinson of Chesterfield.

1775 –   American Revolution begins

The Methodists are holding their meetings in a room above a stable in a yard at the back of the "Old Black's Head" (The Blackamoor's Head).

Wall Bridge Farm, off Newcastle road, exists.

1776 – American Declaration of Independence

Quaker women's meetings are on a sounder footing.

Leek has a postmistress.

1777 – The Caldon Canal is built from Etruria to Froghall.

Under Allwood Wilkinson's will all of his estates pass to his eleven cousins.

Samuel Johnson, visiting Leek, pronounces it to be "*a poor town*".

1778 – Anna Needham, the wife of Joseph Needham, a bookseller, dies on 21 May aged 26.

A room over the stable in the courtyard of the Golden Lion in Church Street is used as a playhouse or club room.

1779 – Death of Captain Cook

1780 – Gordon Riots

There is an organ gallery in St Edward's Church, east of the chancel arch.

The Badnall family's works are engaged in silk dyeing under the management of William's son, Joseph.

A new Congregationalist chapel is built in Derby Street, with a graveyard in front.

Wednesday is the only market day.

Joseph Wardle dies. He leaves an annuity of £5 to be distributed twice a year to the poor of Leek and Lowe township. There is no further reference to this charity.

Fountain Street is linked with Buxton Road along the line of what is to become Osborne Street.

John Davenport inherits Ball Haye in Tittesworth.

The income from the William Grosvenor charity (see 1741) produces £1.

The stalls used at markets and fairs are stored in a building in Derby Street known as the stall barn.

1781 – Again, only two papists returned.

The first Leek Mechanics Institute is formed (NB There is a lot of doubt about this date)

1782 – After the retirement of the Calvinist minister, James Evans, the majority of the members choose a Unitarian, George Chadwick, as their minister. The choice causes a division in the church and a group of thirty-six members call upon Robert Smith to serve them. A lawsuit follows.

William Challinor, who has been articled to John Davenport, becomes his partner.

John Wesley visits Leek for a third time, on 30 March. He preaches to a congregation of some 800 in the parish church on Easter Sunday, in both the morning and the evening. After the evening service there is a Love Feast, described by Wesley as "*such one as I have not seen for many years.*"

1783 – The Quaker Meeting has so declined that they decide to amalgamate with the Stafford monthly meeting. The Leek Friends thereafter hold a preparative meeting.

Thomas Mills, a lawyer, is in partnership with John Cruso.

The income from John Naylor's charity has fallen to £44 3s. 8d., which is then distributed on 23 October.

The wardens engage a man for 5s. a year to enforce the ban on the playing of football in the churchyard.

1784   John Wesley's Deed of Declaration – Charter of Wesleyan Methodism

Bailey's Directory records that there are, in Leek, thirty-five tradespeople and professionals; sixteen in the silk industry; three surgeons; four lawyers; five grocers; two drapers; one druggist; one ironmonger, one fellmonger (i.e. one who prepares skins ready for the tanner); one innkeeper; and one bookseller/printer. There are nine manufacturers and two dyers.

Membership of the Leek Methodist Society numbers thirty. John Wesley visits Leek again, on 23 May.

Five ribbon manufacturers are listed at Leek; two of them also making buttons and silk twist; and there four other makers of buttons and twist, two of them also producing sewing silk.

Robert Smith secures control of the Presbyterian Meeting House in Derby Street. Although a Trinitarian, Smith is not a Presbyterian and under his leadership the Leek church becomes Congregationalist. (A Trinitarian is one who upholds the doctrine of the Trinity. Congregationalism is a form of church government in which each congregation is independent in the management of its own affairs. A Methodist is one who lives his life by the "method", i.e. the regulation of lives and studies.)

Three Leek surgeons are listed: F.B. Fynney, who is also described as an apothecary; and Eli and Isaac Cope. There is also a druggist, Benjamin Challinor.

1785 –   A threedecker pulpit is installed on a new site on the south side of the chancel arch.

The London/Manchester mail coach begins passing through Leek.

The Methodists open a chapel on the east side of Clerk Bank.

Leek Methodist Society is included in the newly created Burslem circuit.

In St Edward's Church, a vestry is built on the north side of the chancel.

John Davenport dies and the practice passes to William Challinor of Pickwood.

The English School is wound up.

1786 –   A man is still being employed to enforce the ban on the playing of football in the churchyard.

The Angel, which has been The Green Dragon, changes its name to The Swan (it is now The Green Dragon again).

Abbey Green Road, which branches north from the Macclesfield road to cross the Churnet at Broad's Bridge, forms part of the road from Leek to Buxton.

Isaac Wilkinson buys out his cousin's interests in three farms in Leek.

A bridge is built over Leek Brook, completed in 1787.

1787 – John Jones is appointed the master of an Anglican Sunday school.

A room over a stable in the courtyard of the Golden Lion in Church Street is being used as a playhouse or club room, and is called The Long Room or The Play Room.

1788 – John Wesley visits Leek on 5 April. He preaches at the Mount Pleasant Chapel, commenting that "*where for many years we seemed to be ploughing upon sand ... at length fruit appears*". Membership now stands at 96.

John Jones, later Leek's pioneer Swedenborgian (a follower of Emanuel Swedenborg, a Swedish religious teacher and founder of the New Jerusalem Church), kept a school.

The William Hulme charity (see 1690) produces an income £1 6s. His son John Hulme's charity produces £1 15s. 10d.

The charity of Thomas Jodrell (see 1728) produces £2 10s.

The income of the charity of John Rothwell (see 1619) is £9 2s. 6d.

Income from Ann Jolliffe's charity (see 1732) is £11 2s.

The charity founded by William Watson (see 1689) produces income of £6.

1789 – The French Revolution begins

Joshua Strangman describes his house on the west side of Spout Street as "*adjoining Holland's well*". He also has the use of a well called Dungeon near the lane later known as Strangman's Walk.

Death of Lord Vane.

John Cruso, son of John Cruso, is born.

Assemblies are held at The Swan.

1790 – Several clockmakers are in Leek, including Thomas Ashton.

An eighth annual fair is added to the existing seven.

Button making declines with the growth of the metalbutton industry in Birmingham but production of ribbons increases.

Samuel Goodwin, a Leek grocer, also makes rope and sacking.

A meeting of commoners is held at the Marquess of Granby inn at Leek. (A "commoner" is not the lowest strata of society and "common land" does not belong to everyone. A commoner is a man who holds the right to pasture a certain number of animals on the common land of the parish. This right is evidently being abused, by some commoners putting more animals on the land than they have a right to, and by others, who have no rights all, putting their animals on the common land.)

Fifteen people with rights in commons and waste of the manors of Leek and Frith sign an agreement to prosecute commoners who overload the commons, and others, without common rights, who put sheep and cattle on commons, the cost to be divided according to the value of each signatory's holding.

Three booksellers are listed in Leek.

Leek manufacturers form an association for the prosecution of felons to protect their stock against theft.

The Quakers have a resident female minister, Hannah West.

Leek is described as a clean town with wide and open streets and a spacious marketplace.

Stone is being quarried at Ballington, south of the town, for road repairs.

1791 – Wilberforce's motion for the abolition of the slave trade is carried through Parliament

The Red Lion in the Market Place is refronted.

John Jones, the master of the Anglican Sunday school, leaves Leek and his school closes.

For two seasons, a theatrical company, led by Samuel Stanton, is based in the town while its theatre at Stafford is being rebuilt. The company includes Harriot Mellon, later to be the Duchess of St Albans. The venue is the assembly room at The Swan. Thomas Entwhistle is the band leader and gives violin and harpsichord lessons.

The right to the fair and market tolls are owned by William Grosvenor's grandson Thomas Fenton Grosvenor and Henry Manifold, the vicar of Brackley, Northants.

A subscription library is formed.

1792 – There are sufficient Methodists to warrant the creation of a circuit for the Leek area alone.

Henry Manifold offered to sell his half share of the right to the market and fair tolls to Thomas Fenton Grosvenor for 1,000 guineas. The offer is rejected.

1793 – Leek is described as being the capital of the Moorlands.

A Grant of £200 is made from Queen Anne's Bounty (a fund created in 1702 to augment the poorer livings of the Church of England) to meet two benefactions of £100 each made that year by Thomas Mills younger and Mrs Pyncombe's trustees. It is used to buy 25 acres in Ipstones.

The Leek association for the prosecution of felons is active.

1794 – Francis Hilliard goes bankrupt. He is described as a bookseller, printer and stationer/ printer at Scolding Bank.

A troop of volunteer cavalry is raised in Leek as part of the Staffordshire Regiment of Gentlemen and Yeomanry.

Foxhunting in the Leek area is organised by the Leek Hunt. Hounds are kept by Richard Badnall, a silk dyer.

Miss M. Nickson advertises her school in Spout Street.

Thomas Ball is dyeing silk in Mill Street.

1795 – Leek's considerable silk industry is producing sewing silks, twist, buttons, silk ferrets (narrow ribbons), shawls and silk handkerchiefs. The industry, *"in which good fortunes have been made"*, employs about 2,000 people living in the town and 1,000 in the neighbourhood.

The church is now without a spire.

John Condlyffe is in charge of the law practice.

Mail coaches run between London and Manchester daily through Leek in each direction from the George in Spout Street. In addition, coaches run twice a week to London from The Swan in Spout Street, and three times a week between Manchester and Birmingham in each direction from the Wilkes's Head in Spout Street.

1796 – Stone from Leek Moor is used for walling.

1797 – Thomas Mills, the son of William Mills, is born – later to be Sheriff of Staffordshire.

Mount Pleasant Methodist chapel opens a Sunday school.

Ball Haye Hall is rebuilt with stone from Upper Hulme.

An Act of Parliament authorises a reservoir at Rudyard to feed the Caldon Canal.

An additional fair is held on the Wednesday after 10 October.

A shade behind the Buffalo's Head is used for stretching and drying silk as well as mohair.

Charles Ball, a Leek Methodist, begins to hold a Sunday school in his house. Numbers soon become too great for the house.

The Methodists establish a nondenominational Sunday school and the Anglicans cooperate in the work.

1798 – Miss Fynney keeps a boarding school for girls.

John Ashton is the only clock and watchmaker recorded.

Leek surgeons are listed: F.B. Fynney, who is also described as an apothecary; and Eli and Isaac Cope are listed again. Fynney is also described as a surgeon and a man midwife. The fourth surgeon is George Cope.

1799 – Mills and Cruso, solicitors, make their clerk, Henry Jones, a junior partner.

William Condlyffe dies. His son John is confined as a lunatic. The practice lapses in a few years.

THE NINETEENTH CENTURY

1800 – The churchyard of St Edward's Church is extended on the north side by 868 square yards.

Nearly three acres of Leek moor on Ashbourne Road are inclosed as a garden for the workhouse.

Charles Ball is a Leek Methodist and the Sunday school has 200 pupils.

A Coventry man, Thomas Horton, introduces the weaving of figured ribbons in Leek.

There are references to other silk weavers in the town.

Twisting continued longer than weaving as a domestic industry or one carried out in shades and not part of the mills.

Thomas Ball, working in a shade behind St Edward's Church, introduces the twisting of sewing silk by means of a "gate". After the silk has been wound and doubled by women and children, it goes to a *twister working gate*. Here the threads are twisted, attached to a gate and wound onto bobbins. Each twister employs a boy, known as a helper or trotter. His job is to take the rod carrying the bobbins and run some 25 yards to the other end of the shade. There he passes the thread around the "cross" and runs back to the gate. He then repeats the operation until the thread has reached the required thickness.

William Challinor dies and the law practice is carried on by his partner George Ridgway Killmister.

1801 – The sexton is paid 5 shillings for ringing the curfew.

Charles Ball, a Leek Methodist, now has a Sunday school of 300 pupils, of whom twenty-two are being taught to write. The school moves successively to Mount Pleasant Methodist chapel, to the grammar school and to the Assembly Room at the Swan inn.

The population of Leek and Lowe is 3,489.

The Trent and Mersey Canal Company opens a branch canal running from the Caldon Canal, east of Endon, to a basin and wharf on Newcastle Road in Leek and crossing the River Churnet by an aqueduct.

A tollhouse is built near the canal wharf.

1802 – Napoleon becomes First Consul – An Act of Parliament seeks to protect the Health and Morals of Apprentices, and regulates factories

The Countess of Stamford leaves Westwood to her son Booth Grey, who himself then dies this year and is succeeded by his son, also called Booth.

A new association for the prosecution of felons is formed covering the townships of Leek and Lowe, Leekfrith and Tittesworth.

William Travis starts on his own account as a clockmaker in Market Place.

1803 – French prisoners of war arrive in Leek, which is a designated Parole Town.

Eleven friendly societies exist in Leek, with a membership of 485. Most of them are associated with inns.

One charity received a further £25 from land at Oulton, in Rushton Spencer, partly as interest on money from sale of timber and partly from further occasional sales of timber and underwood.

Pickfords' wagons between London and Manchester are coming through Leek.

A twoday race meeting on Leek Moor is advertised for the Monday and Tuesday after the third Sunday in October.

A.J. Worthington & Co. originates as James Goostrey & Co.

Joseph Badnall dies and the dye-works are taken over by his son William and his brother James.

1804 – Napoleon becomes Emperor of France

Jean Baptiste François Mien and General Jean Baptiste Brunet arrive in Leek as French prisoners of war (POWs).

On 12 June the Staffordshire Regiment of Gentlemen and Yeomanry are supplemented by a troop of infantry.

The Leek meeting of the Quakers commends Henry Bowman and his family to a Quaker meeting at Oswego in New York state.

The farmhouse called Westwood is offered for sale with 212 acres as "*a pleasant and convenient country residence*".

1805 – Battle of Trafalgar

A "cucking stool" stands by the River Churnet off Abbey Green Road near Broad's Bridge and has apparently been on this site since the 1560s. A chair, which may have been part of the cucking stool, was later kept in St Edward's Church until it was stolen.

There is a well on the south side of Ashbourne Road; Well Street, running north from Ashbourne Road, may derive its name from this well.

The Leek Inclosure Act is passed confirming the Earl of Macclesfield's ownership of the waterworks as the lord of the manor.

A new fire engine, called the *Lord of the Manor*, is given by the Earl of Macclesfield.

The town and the places adjoining it are supplied with water piped from two reservoirs on Leek Moor, at what are now the north end of Mount Road and the east end of Fountain Street.

The income from Ann Jolliffe's charity (see 1732) produces £38 10s.

The charity English school ceases to function.

1806 – The Market Cross is moved from the south end of the Market Square to Cornhill on the Cheddleton Road.

The old Town Hall is built on the site. This hall is designed and built by Robert Emerson, a joiner, and John Radford, a stonemason. The building consists of a basement with two lockups. The ground floor was originally kept open for use by market people who found it dark and inconvenient and eventually abandoned it.

The existing lockup in the town is pulled down when the Town Hall in the Market Place is built containing two cells.

Thomas Mills has sold his interest in the law firm to Mr Cruso.

F.B. Fynney dies. He built Compton House on the Cheddleton Road.

William Badnall, a Leek silk dyer, dies. He leaves interest on £1,000 to be distributed in blankets, quilts, clothing and other necessities such as coal, but not food or drink, on 5 November, to twenty poor widows aged sixty or over; half of the widows to be residents in Leek town and half in Lowe. On his death the partnership is formed between James Badnall, his brother Richard Badnall and his son Joseph Badnall.

1807 – England abolishes the slave trade

Cruso and Jones, solicitors, take on Sinckler (St Clair?) Porter of Lichfield as a partner.

George Ridgway Killmister goes into partnership with William Challinor's eldest son, also William.

A gallery over the south aisle in St Edward's Church is mentioned.

The English school has definitely ceased because the annuity expires (See 1786)

A friendly society is established at The Swan (one of many such schemes in town).

1808 – Houses are built to the north of St Edward's Church. They became known as Petty France. They are built by James Fernyhough. The name Petty France may derive from the area where (some?) of the POWs resided or from the proximity of that part of the churchyard where several of them are buried.

Richard Cutting, a silk manufacturer, and a Sergeant in the Leek Loyal Volunteers, is appointed as the Superintendent of the Methodist Sunday School (a position he will hold until his death in 1856).

John Cruso is the Cornet, the officer who carries the colours, of the Leek Yeomanry.

1809 – *Holden's Directory* lists nine manufacturers and two dyers in the town.

Hannah West, the Quakers' resident female minister, dies.

Thomas Ball is still in business dyeing silk in Mill Street.

1810 – The governor of the workhouse is paid a salary of £42 per year and the matron one of £10.

A wake is held on the third Sunday in October, possibly in association with the Feast of the Translation of Edward the Confessor (13 October), who is then regarded as the patron saint of the parish church.

Spout Street is the main residential street with several large houses. Derby Street has a few large houses and several smaller ones. Stockwell Street has about thirty houses

Six children at a time are being taught for free at the Grammar School. Any attempt to maintain a purely classical syllabus has long been abandoned.

Louis Gerard, an emigré priest at Cobridge in Burslem, says mass at Leek for the French prisoners of war and the Irish workers. The usual place is a room in Pickwood Road.

Emma Neau, daughter of Francis Neau (a French POW) and a lady named Margaret(?) is born.

John Condlyffe, a solicitor, confined as a lunatic, dies.

1811 – Leek Moor is inclosed.

The vicar is assigned 8½ acres in respect of his glebe and in lieu of the tithe corn and rents from 20 acres.

The population of Leek and Lowe is 3,703.

The Town Lands, that part of Leek Moor which remained common waste, are inclosed under the Act of 1805 and vested in seven freeholders as trustees who are to manage them and keep accounts. In addition five acres on Leek Moor, east of the town, are assigned to them.

The Leek inclosure award replaces the rent charge with just over one acre of land at the junction of Mount Road and Kniveden Lane.

There are 178 Methodists.

A new chapel is built at Mount Pleasant with a graveyard attached. The old chapel is converted into houses. The French POW, Jean Bapstiste Nillot, dies, aged 43, at 6 Petty France.

John Brough is in business in the silk trade.

1812 – **Napoleon invades Russia**

Charles Luneaud, of Petty France, shoots and kills Captain Decourbed in a duel.

Leek is one of the small industrial towns where Sunday schools proved to be popular with workers and provided most of the formal education in the town

The small porch to St Edward's Church is erected on the south side of the chancel.

The last of the French POWs arrive in Leek. They are a changing population and at any one time there are about 140 in the town. Two companies of militia and a squadron of yeomanry are assigned to guard the prisoners. They enjoy considerable freedom, on parole to stay within a radius of one mile from the Market Place. They are welcomed into local society.

1813 – James Badnall dies.

Robert Hobson has opened a day and boarding school for boys on Clerk Bank.

In St Edward's Church there is a gallery over the north aisle.

The younger Booth sells the Birchall estate to John Davenport, a potter and glassmaker of Longport and native of Leek.

The Methodists establish a nondenominational Sunday school, controlled by the Wesleyan Methodists.

The Anglicans set up their own Sunday school on the Madras system (whereby the older children are taught and they in turn teach the younger ones). One hundred children join it from the nondenominational Sunday school. It is held in the grammar school and supported by subscriptions plus collections at St Edward's Church.

1814 – The capital of the Thomas Birtles charity is used to buy stock.

A fair on the first Wednesday in January is introduced but is later changed to the last Wednesday in December.

1815 – **Battle of Waterloo**

West Street School opens as a Wesleyan Sunday school.

Thomas Mills is born, the son of William Mills (later Sheriff of Staffordshire). He is to die aged eighteen, leaving no heir.

There is a pinfold (or "penfold", a pound where straying cattle and sheep are detained) in Spout Street at the junction with Sheepmarket.

French Graves

Stocks for the punishment of offenders stand near the Town Hall until their removal to a site beneath Overton Bank. As a replacement, steel stocks are set up in the Market Place opposite the Red Lion.

There is a Post Office in the Market Place.

James Bostock is born in 13 Church Street (he is later with the Bostock and Wombwell travelling menagerie).

Quarrying is taking place at Kniveden.

There are more than 100 weavers in the town.

Eight pinnacles are placed on the tower of St Edward's Church.

John Brough is in partnership with Mr Baddeley with premises in Stockwell Street.

Land at Barngates is advertised as being a suitable site for a large factory.

The chapel at "Lower End", at the bottom of Mill Street, is registered for "Particular Baptists".

A total of over 3,400 French POWs have been in Leek (not all at the same time!), but most have now left with the coming of peace. Some have married locally and stayed.

1816 – In St Edward's Church, the gallery over the north aisle is altered.

The vestry in St Edward's Church has fallen down and been rebuilt.

Distress funds are established by public subscription for the support of the workhouse.

Leek manufacturers' association for the prosecution of felons is active.

A mill in Mill Street is using steam power.

1817 – The ground floor of the Town Hall in Market Place is converted into a newsroom. The upper room is used for meetings. The cost is met by subscribers, shareholders and (for lockups) the County Quarter Sessions. The building is too small to be of much use for public gatherings and is considered to be architecturally undistinguished.

The Wesleyans' schoolroom in West Street is advertised as nondenominational. It has 536 pupils, including nineteen adults.

Jones and Porter have separate practices in Leek.

Cruso has taken his son John into partnership and his soninlaw Charles Coupland, a Leek attorney, joins the partnership too.

Compton is so named.

There is a slump and prices and wages have fallen.

Four hundred workers from Manchester arrive at Leek on their way to London to present their grievances to the Government. They are known as the "*Blanketeers*" from the blankets which they carry with them. They are not allowed to stay in Leek and continue towards Ashbourne. A few hours after their departure, Edward Powys, the incumbent of Cheddleton and a magistrate, calls out the Leek troop of yeomanry and goes in pursuit. He catches up with them at Mayfield and disperses them. They try to return to Leek but only about thirty succeed. They are escorted to Macclesfield by 400 special constables sworn in by Powys.

1818 – The inn at the south of the Market Square is still known as the Blackamoor's Head.

Two brothers, Samuel and William Phillips, are silk manufacturers at Barngates. They live in the house known as The Field.

There are two gardeners and seedsmen in town.

There is in existence the Volunteer Watch (a group of men armed men with cudgels etc. who are paid to patrol the streets to see that the peace is kept), which assembles at the Town Hall in the Market Place.

Six surgeons are listed, including three members of the Fynney family.

Druggists mentioned are Benjamin and Jesse Challinor, and John Smith.

There is just one factory, which has only a few looms, in Mill Street. It is run by Richard Badnall and William Laugharn.

About 200 ribbon weavers are working engine looms and about 100 are working single handlooms. In addition, there are between fifty and sixty broadsilk weavers, producing handkerchiefs, shawls and silk, varying in breadth between 18 inches and 1½ yards.

John Davenport begins improvements to Westwood Hall.

Parsons and Bradshaw's Directory lists fifteen manufacturers and two dyers.

Coaches run daily to London, Birmingham and Manchester.

The Red Lion in Market Place and The Roebuck in Derby Street are the main coaching inns.

John Ashton, father and son, are clockmakers in Sheepmarket.

Eight joiners and cabinetmakers are recorded

Ralph Mountfort works as a rope and twine maker in Derby Street. There are four rope and twine makers in the town.

There are two forges in Leek producing edge tools.

William Hope is a bookseller, stationer and bookbinder in Custard Street.

Charles Cane is a bookseller and stationer in Sheepmarket.

John Smith is a bookseller and druggist in the Market Place.

The Post Office is in Spout Street.

Francis Hilliard is a printer on Scalding Bank (now Overton Bank). He is also Parish Clerk.

1819 – John Cruso buys the house later known as Foxlowe from Thomas Mills.

The Humane Society (a friendly society) is established as a benefit society for men. It quickly folds. Most friendly societies are tavern-based but some, which function only as sickness and burial clubs, did not socialise in public houses.

Foxlowe

A separate association for the prosecution of felons is formed for Leekfrith.

1820 – **George IV**

What is later to be known as the California Mills is built. It sees the concentration of all manufacturing processes on a single site. Standing in Horton Street it was later claimed to be the oldest brick textile mill in the north of England.

The town is expanding on all sides. There is dissatisfaction with the ministry of James Morrow on pastoral rather than doctrinal grounds, and this causes some members to attend the Methodist services.

The Leek Manufacturers' Association for the Prosecution of Felons is still in existence.

The Court of Leek and Frith appoints the headborough, who is the head of the frankpledge (a mutual suretyship by which the members of a tithing are made responsible for one another) and the tithing (district of ten householders each responsible for the actions of the others) for a decennary (period of ten years) for Heaton, and the headborough and pinner (also spelled "pinder": one responsible for impounding straying cattle) for Rushton Spencer.

The partnership of Cruso, Jones and Porter, solicitors, is dissolved.

The Court Leet is held at the Red Lion in Leek every October before the Earl of Macclesfield's steward.

The Manor Court appoints two scavengers (street cleaners) for the township of Leek and Lowe. It also orders a 5s. fine for anyone depositing filth, ashes or rubbish in the streets of the town or on the highways or footpaths of the manor and failing to remove such deposits within three days after notice from the scavengers.

Absentees from the Court who have not essoined (put forward a good reason for their absence) are fined 6d. each and an order is made for the compilation of a full list of suitors in time for the next court.

The Court appoints a Constable, a Deputy Constable and a Headborough for the whole manor, combining the roles of beadle (Originally "mace-bearer" but latterly an officer of the parish with the power to punish petty offenders), "bang beggar" (officer responsible for locking up vagrants and beggars causing a public nuisance) and pinner for Leek and Lowe (with rise in salary from 1s. to 3s. a week "*in case he executes his duty properly*"); two market lookers (officers responsible for conduct at the markets), a pinner for Leekfrith and a headborough for Lowe, besides the officials for Heaton and Rushton.

There are buildings along Buxton and Ashbourne roads; also Cross Street and Well Street. There are also a few buildings in Fountain Street itself.

Monthly cheese fairs are being held.

Despite competition from metal buttons, the production of handmade buttons persists. Large quantities of "*Florentine buttons*" are being made by several hundred women and children in the surrounding villages. "Florentine buttons" is a name coined by Joshua Brough for buttons covered in drab silk cloth with a linen back, mounted on moulds of wood, bone or iron.

The former Blackamoor's Head is known as the Black's Head.

Albion Street and King Street are being built.

Weaving is organised by "*undertakers*" (i.e. middlemen: those who "undertake" to provide goods to one person and get them from another) owning a number of looms and employing journeymen (workers who are paid by the day, from the French *jour* = "day") and apprentices. The work is carried out on the second floors of buildings over groups of two or more houses, with the space being lit by elongated windows and ventilated by means of sliding frames. The undertaker would live in one of the houses. There are many examples of this type of building in Leek.

The distribution from John Naylor's charity is usually made every two years in the form of tickets for food or clothing, to be used in Leek shops.

A pack of hounds called the Moorland Foxhounds hunts the country which covers Leek, Biddulph and Draycottinthe-Moors.

The town's silk industry continues to develop and the first mills are established.

1821 – The partnership of John Brough and Baddeley is dissolved and John Brough continues to run the business alone.

Stock is purchased with the money left for charity by Rebecca Lowe in 1765 and produces an income of £13 1s. 7½d. By then the weekly dole of 2s. 6d. has for some time been paid to each almswoman but there is not enough money to provide new gowns as directed by the foundress, but it is hoped that there will be enough to buy some in 1825.

The population of Leek and Lowe is 4,855.

William Challinor is born at Pickwood Hall on 10 March.

Fred Hill prints *A Selection of Psalms and Hymns for the Cheddleton Church.*

The monthly cheese fairs are reduced to three a year, in March, September and November.

1822 – William Grosvenor's Charity has been lost.

The vicar distributes the dole weekly in the form of sixteen quarts of soup to eight poor widows or families in Leek and Lowe township.

The charity founded by William Watson (see 1689) produces income of £15 10s.

Under Thomas Birtles' charity there is a distribution of £5 given to poor widows.

The sum of £10 7s. 6d., the income of the charity of John Rothwell (see 1619), is distributed by the vicar in a weekly dole to six poor widows.

The cattle market is held every alternate Wednesday from 28 July until Christmas.

Several charities for the poor, which have been managed by the churchwardens of Leek, are merged as the Town Dole. It is uncertain whether some of earliest charities are intended to benefit the whole of the ancient parish or only the township of Leek and Lowe or the town of Leek. However, the area is restricted to the Leek and Lowe township.

The income from all charities, together with that from the charity of Anne Jolliffe, produces £85 12s. 10d. which is distributed in money, blankets and linen at Christmas; coal is also sometimes given. To prevent people who live outside of the Leek and Lowe township receiving any benefit, those eligible to share in the distribution are issued with tickets.

Land at Oulton, in Rushton Spencer, is left for charitable purposes and let at £25 year.

John Jones, the Leek schoolmaster, registers his schoolroom, behind the Black's Head inn in Derby Street, for worship by Protestant dissenters.

William Hilliard joins his father in the printing business.

Richard Bentley dies. He is the last vicar to add to the library.

Condliffe's practice is being carried on by Joseph's son William.

The dole is given in sums of one shilling or less by the tenant of the land; prior notice of distribution having been given by the town crier.

Meetings of leading inhabitants are held to discuss the setting up of a bank.

The vicarage is enlarged by T.H. Heathcote after his institution as vicar.

From the charity of William Mills (see 1749), the poor's share is £3 15s. which together with £2 15s. from James Rudyard's charity is spent on a weekly dole of thirty-six bread rolls distributed by the organblower after the Sunday morning service. Between six and eight rolls are taken to poor people too old to attend church.

Because an insufficient number of poor people from Lowe are eligible under the charity of William Badnall (see 1806), the number of town widows who benefit is increased to thirteen.

The garret of a house in King Street belonging to William Ward, solicitor, is sometimes used for Roman Catholic services.

1823 – Six dwellings in what later becomes Wood Street are built by William Thompson, a broadsilk weaver. Four of the dwellings are built as two backtoback pairs and have a workshop on the top floor which is not integrated with the living accommodation but has its own staircase and external door.

Anthony Ward and Co. has ten machines in the Albion Mill in Albion Street.

The charity of Thomas Jolliffe and Mrs Haywood. (see 1723) produces £27 5s. Leek Savings Bank is established and uses the lower room in the old Town Hall in Market Place. It is open between noon and 1 p.m. at first every Monday and later two Mondays a month.

A silk mill opens in Workhouse Street. (later Brook Street).

John Wrexford opens a mill in London Street.

1824 – The scold's bridle is last used.

The churchyard of St Edward's Church is increased by half an acre.

Charles Coupland leaves the Cruso partnership.

Charles Flint, surgeon, moves from Stockwell Street to Compton House.

Hope Mill, in Fountain Street, has been established by Thomas Carr and Co.

Land at Ipstones is owed by the Vicar of Leek and is let for £18.

William Hammersley opens the silkdyeing works at Bridge End. The Hammersley firm is to remain in business in Mill Street and Bridge End until the early 20th century.

The first known building society in Leek, Leek Building Society, is formed, with forty-two shares to be paid for at a rate of one guinea per month over six years. Each subscriber is entitled to a house worth £80. Land is bought at Ball Haye Green, and it is arranged that fifteen houses should be built there during the summer of 1824.

The Leek Building Society begins the erection of forty-two houses on the north side of Haregate Road at Ball Haye Green.

The Charity Commissioners visit Leek, find the town's charities generally in good order but suggest some improvements in management.

1825 – A body of thirty-four Improvement Commissioners is established by an Act of Parliament to light, watch, cleanse and improve the town of Leek. The town is defined as a circle with 1,200 yards' radius measured from the hall in Market Place plus much of the Leek and Lowe township area and parts of Leekfrith and Tittesworth. The Improvement Commissioners are empowered to appoint watchmen and pay them, and they duly appoint four of them, each with a watch box.

The rights to the fair and the market tolls are owned by William Grosvenor and Henry Townsend.

A fortnightly cattle market is introduced during part of the year and new fairs are started.

The Commercial Bank opens in the Market Place, the partnership consisting of Richard Badnall of Highfield House in Leekfrith, his son Richard of Ashenhurst in Bradnop, R.R. Ellis, Henry Cruso and F.G. Spilsbury All of them, except Ellis, are connected with the silk industry.

Richard Cooper, a staunch Wesleyan Methodist who was born at Cheddleton in 1803, is admitted to Membership of the Royal College of Surgeons.

Princess Victoria, aged six, drives through Leek on a carriage journey from Buxton to Trentham.

Leek Grammar School offers "*classical, mathematical, and commercial instruction*". The school could support both a master and an usher (an under-teacher) but only if one or both has other employment.

Albion Street and King Street are laid out, consisting mainly of silk weavers' cottages.

The Cock Inn opens in Derby Street.

The easing of duties on imported silk and manufactured goods leads to further depression.

The increasing use of steam power in silk weaving means a growth in the number of factories and a decline in domestic working.

The Bank of Fowler, Haworth and Gaunt is situated in the Market Place, in the building on the corner of the Market Place and Stockwell Street, formerly the Cock Inn.

1826 – A foreign visitor notes that "*stone houses with gable windows decorated with balls and acroteria* (ornamentation at the top of a pedestal), *thatched roof above. Brick buildings with attractive mouldings and brick gables.*" He also describes the silk mill in Mill Street as "*a fine factory building, at the end of the town, quite new, the most splendid position in the whole place.*" He makes sketches of spinning apparatus, which he also describes in detail.

The Wesleyans' schoolroom in West Street has over 900 children attending.

A group is constituted as the Leek Gas Light Co. They buy land on the west side of Newcastle Road, and J.A. West of Durham, engineer and chief shareholder, builds the gasworks there.

The dye-works of the Badnall family is run by a partnership consisting of Richard's son, also Richard, F.G. Spilsbury and Henry Cruso. The partners also manufacture silk and silk machinery. The partnership is dissolved and is bought by James Badnall's son, Joseph.

Cornelius Brumby, who has been an usher at the grammar school, opens his own school. He publishes locally his own system of shorthand.

The Salop Fire Office pays £5 a year towards the cost of repairing the engine, with two other offices contributing £2 10s. each.

Ball Haye Street, Queen Street, Earl Street and another King Street (later called Regent Street) have been laid out.

1827 – An Act of Parliament obliges Lord Macclesfield and his heirs to supply the town with water from the reservoirs. It allows him to charge up to £5 a year for each house supplied, according to its rented or rateable value. People requiring water for commercial purposes have to agree a charge with the Earl.

The gasworks is opened on Newcastle Road by Leek Gas Light Co.

The open space at the east end of Derby Street is bought by the Trustees of Town Lands from the Earl of Macclesfield, as a site for a fire-engine house. The land soon comes to be used for a cattle market, and in 1840s the fire engine is kept in rented premises.

The coach between Manchester and Nottingham runs daily in each direction from The Swan.

The manors of Leek and Frith are described as covering the townships of Leek and Lowe, and Leekfrith and Tittesworth manors. However, the manor retained some vestigial control over Heaton and Rushton Spencer

A second printer in town, George Nall, sets up a press in Spout Street.

An agreement is made by the Gas Company with the Improvement Commissioners to light about 100 public lamps at £2 year each from 29 September to 5 April. The lamps are to be lit from dusk, half until 2 a.m. and the rest until 6 a.m. No lights are to be lit for the three nights before full moon and one night after it. There is also to be a private supply to houses, factories and shops. The dial of the clock in St Edward's church tower is also lit.

The Revd. T.H. Heathcote enlarges the vicarage at his own expense.

James Jeffries, a priest at Cheadle, starts to say mass in Leek, in Mr Ward's house in King Street, with a congregation of fifteen or sixteen.

1828 – Father James Jeffries begins to build a Roman Catholic chapel on the corner of Fountain Street and Portland Street. It is built by a Cheadle builder named Higgs, at a cost of £700.

Assemblies are still being held at The Swan.

The Albion Mill is completed.

A chapel is built at the corner of Ball Haye Street and Regent Street. The building was originally intended for use as a Wesleyan Sunday school only, but it is fitted with a gallery and an organ at the expense of James Wardle and also used for services.

Francis Hilliard, the bookseller, is still in business.

The annual procession of Sunday school children is first recorded. It takes place on the last Sunday in August. About 1,000 children from the Wesleyan Methodist Sunday schools walk that day, and hymns are sung in the Market Place.

Robert Hobson, or another member of his family, is still running a boys' school on Clerk Bank.

The subscription library is refounded as the Leek Book Society, with membership restricted to thirty.

Wesleyans have the most Sunday school pupils, with over 1,000 on roll at their two schools.

1829 – Parliament creates a Police Force in London

All forty-two houses planned to have been built in Haregate Road by the Leek Building Society have been completed and the Society is disbanded.

A large part of the Congregationalist congregation, with the support of the Congregationalist ministers of Staffordshire, secede to form a new church. The seceders first meet in a room behind the Black's Head inn in Derby Street.

John Brough moves his premises to Union Street, where he builds a house next to his silk warehouse there. He was living in Tittesworth.

Father James Jeffries opens the Roman Catholic chapel at the corner of Fountain Street and Portland Street. The Earl of Shrewsbury contributed £130 towards the cost of £700. Dedicated to St Mary, it includes an altarpiece depicting the Virgin and Child by Joseph Barney and four paintings of saints brought from Lisbon by Brigittine nuns who later settled at Aston Hall in Stone. Father Jeffries said Mass on Monday morning, arriving from Cheadle on Sunday evening to stay with Henry Bermingham in London Road.

At Ball Haye Green, a fortnightly Sunday Methodist service is held.

Two Sunday services are being held in the Regent Street Methodist Chapel.

Two friendly societies, one for men and the other for women, celebrate the feast day on the first Friday in August, when members walk through town, attend a sermon in St Edward's Church, and then have separate dinners in the Swan and the Red Lion inns.

Ralph Mountfort is still making rope and twine in the Market Place. There are now only three rope and twine makers in the town.

West Street exists.

The Post Office has moved to Spout Street (later St Edward Street).

A new bridge is built across the River Churnet on the Congleton Road, near the old bridge.

James Morrow, the minister of the Derby Street Congregational Chapel, opens a boys' school, the Derby Street Academy, in a schoolroom built on to the chapel.

Joseph Howard is a tinman (dealer in tinware), brazier and ironmonger at 24 Market Place. He also breeds greyhounds.

The combined Staffordshire Regiment of Gentlemen and Yeomanry and the Troop of Infantry is disbanded.

Union Street and New Street are laid out by four silk manufacturers who have premises there. The street linking them is called New Street.

1830 – William IV

Another dye-works is established by Joshua Wardle on Leek Brook near its confluence with the River Churnet.

Swedenborgians meet occasionally in a schoolroom behind The Black's Head inn in Derby Street.

Silk weavers' cottages have been built in London Street.

The Lowe Hill tollhouse is sold after a new line of the road is built to the south. It survives as part of a house.

Joshua Wardle's son, Thomas, claims that the water of the River Churnet is among the best dyeing water in Europe. In particular it produces a unique ravenblack dye for which Leek is to become celebrated. It is so called because its rich blueblack resembles the bluest part of a raven's feathers.

The death of Joseph Badnall. His dyeing business passes to his sister Ann. She lets the works to John Clowes.

A threestoreyed shade in Clerk Bank, with four gates (twisted chimneys) on each floor, is offered for sale.

Leek is described as one of the handsomest market towns in Staffordshire.

Cliffe Park Hall is built at the northern end of Rudyard Lake. It later becomes the club house for a golf club and later still a youth hostel.

Several friendly societies meet at other inns in the town.

Petty Sessions are held at The Swan every alternate Wednesday.

Jodrell's Chapel in St Edward's Church is described as an ancient canopied pew which is claimed by the occupiers of the estates formerly belonging to Dieulacres abbey. It contains eight seats.

Congregationalists form a Sunday school.

Friendly societies parade carrying banners which display their emblems, accompanied by a band.

1831 – The population of Leek and Lowe is 6,374.

Thomas Wardle is born, son of Joshua Wardle, whose dyeing business is at Leekbrook.

Jurors assemble at the eleven-acre meadow and, after being sworn in, carry out "*a minute inspection of the town*", making presentments of nuisances and encroachments. (This is a survival of the origin of the jury system when the members of the jury gave their decision not from evidence presented to them but from their own personal knowledge.) They return about 4 p.m. for "*an ample and excellent dinner*" and afterwards appoint the officers for the following year. The officials appointed consist of constable and deputy, headborough and deputy, two market lookers, and beadle, bang beggar and pinner. A combined bailiff of court and scavenger is appointed and two overseers of highways for the town of Leek are reappointed.

A Board of Health is formed by the leading inhabitants in case of a cholera outbreak in town. Poor families are visited and their needs ascertained. The sum of £110 is raised by subscription and distributed in bedding and coal.

Isaac Wilkinson dies. His heir, George Yeldham Ricketts, under terms of the will, takes the name of Wilkinson.

John Brough's sons, Joshua and James, enter into a partnership as Joshua and James Brough and Co.

Friendly societies parade on the last Thursday in July. The town's factories close for the day.

George Nall is a distributor (?) at the Stamp Office in the Sheepmarket.

1832 – **First Reform Act enfranchises the upper middle classes**

The mill of James Goosetry, in Portland Street, is described as new when it is offered for sale. Soon afterwards, the business is taken over by James Hammond and Henry Turner.

At the workhouse, the number of inmates averages fifty-four, maintained and clothed for 3s. 6d. each per week. The children are sent out to work in the silk mills.

A dispensary is established to provide medical and surgical help for the industrious working classes in their homes and attendance on poor married women during their confinements.

The Board of Health is legally constituted. It hires a building as a cholera hospital in case of need. Only one death in the town is recorded.

Jeremiah Barnes is appointed the Master of Leek Grammar School, and is also employed as the usher/organist at St Edward's Church, where he is the assistant curate.

A resident Roman Catholic priest is appointed.

There are four surgeons listed. This is a number which the vicar, T.H. Heathcote, considers to be too few for a town the size of Leek. They include Charles Flint, one of those listed in 1818.

The buildings on the opposite side of Haregate Road are completed.

An amateur performance takes place at what is called The Theatre Royal, which occupied premises at the Red Lion.

George Nall, printer, moves to Sheepmarket, and introduces copperplate printing. He also trades as a bookseller and stationer.

The Methodist Chapel in Regent Street is known as the Brunswick Chapel.

Methodist services at Ball Haye Green have ceased.

1833 – **The Factories Act provides that children under thirteen are allowed to work only ten hours a day**

The Congregationalists divide. One group moves to a stable behind the Black's Head, and they later move to their own buildings in Union Street (later the site of the Majestic Cinema) (but see also 1829).

Racing takes place on the Monday and Tuesday after the third Sunday in October (21 and 22 October) on a course at Birchall Dale on the west side of Cheddleton Road.

John Clowes dies, and the Badnall dye-works are let to William Hammersley, a former employee of Richard Badnall.

A wake is held on the third Sunday in October, possibly in association with the Feast of Translation of Edward the Confessor (13 October), then regarded as patron saint of the parish church.

The Old Methodist Chapel on Mount Pleasant starts to be used by the circuit's preachers.

The Leek subbranch of the Hanley branch of the Manchester and Liverpool District Bank is established. At first it opens on Wednesdays only.

The friendly societies parade on the last Thursday in July. Celebrations continue on the Friday.

1834 – The son of Francis Hilliard, William Michael Hilliard, has taken over the bookselling business with premises in Church Street.

Jeremiah Barnes, the assistant curate at St Edward's and master of the grammar school, starts a monthly lecture at the school. It so well attended that he begins to give a lecture and a service in church every Sunday evening later the same year.

The Improvement Commissioners are paying £7 year for each gas light.

Hobson's school on Clerk Bank is closed.

Portland Street, between Fountain Street and Buxton Road, exists.

The Manchester and Liverpool District Bank opens daily.

The ceded Congregationalists open their chapel in Union Street.

James Goostrey is a silk manufacturer, in Portland Street.

Lord Macclesfield gives part of the Grammar School's playground as a site; money is raised by subscription and grants from the government and from the National Society; and a twostoreyed brick building with stone dressings and some Gothic fenestration is erected to the design of William Rawlins. The Trustees of Town Lands are authorised to admit poor children from Leek or any other place within two miles of Leek parish.

A Sunday school is connected with St Mary's Roman Catholic Chapel in Fountain Street.

There is unrest in the town. Attempts by handloom weavers to defend and improve their rates of pay for piecework lead to a strike. A shortlived silk operatives' union has been formed by May, when over 400 men and women march through the town with considerable ceremony at the funeral of a fellow member. A local band leads the cortège.

The Post Office is moved to Custard Street (later Stanley Street).

The December Fair has become a Hiring Fair (where farm labourers, domestics etc. offer their services to the highest bidder for the coming year. It was also a fair where children were offered by parents as servants.)

The castiron mileposts on Ashbourne Road are inserted. They are still there.

The Commissioners' police force consists of a Superintendent (who is also Clerk to the Commissioners and Clerk to the Gas Light Co.), four constables and some watchmen.

A subscription library is run by George Nall, printer and bookseller in Sheepmarket.

Over 1,000 suitors usually attended the Court Leet.

The chapel at the bottom of Mill Street, for Particular Baptists, no longer exists.

King Street (the second one of that name!) is renamed Regent Street.

Ralph Mountfort, the rope and twine maker, is based in Custard (later Stanley) Street at the premises later to be the grocers, Mountford Johnson & Co (now the bookshop).

White's Directory lists thirty-one manufacturers.

The theatre at The Swan is still in use.

There are four gardeners in town

The workhouse has been enlarged to four storeys and measures 75 feet in length and 21 feet in depth.

Westwood Hall is "*a neat mansion with extensive plantations and pleasure grounds*". John Davenport has added a new south entrance front and a wing to the north-east, employing James Elmes as architect. The enlarged house is two storeys with attics, in Elizabethan style with curved gables and mullioned and transomed windows.

George Nall, the printer in Spout Street, is joined by his son, Robert.

Five newly built houses in Blackamoor's Head Lane (later Pickwood Road) are advertised for sale along with a silk shade extending over them. A shade might occupy the top floor over several houses.

A branch of the Manchesterbased Commercial Bank of England is opened in Derby Street.

1835 – A new Sunday school is opened on the site of the Grammar School, with a salaried master and mistress, thirty-four monitors, and 265 children (141 girls and 124 boys). The unusual predominance of girls over boys may have arisen because the mistress as well as the master is allowed to teach writing.

Horton Street Mill is occupied by Glendinning and Gaunt.

There are, in the town, seven mills (one unoccupied), with 119 power looms, employing 744 people, 477 of them female.

The Wesleyans have almost 1,000 pupils at Sunday Schools.

Benjamin Barlow is appointed as the organist and choirmaster at St Edward's Church.

A coach runs to Macclesfield three times a week from the Roebuck.

A subscription is started to meet the cost of Jeremiah Barnes's weekly lecture, including a stipend of £30 year for the lecturer. In addition, a special sermon is preached annually to raise funds. Barnes also starts "Cottage Lectures".

Derby Street

The Roman Catholic congregation appears to have declined in numbers.

A Charity Ball is held at The Swan.

After his appointment as the choirmaster and organist at St Edward's Church, Benjamin Barlow encourages the development of music in the town.

Joshua Wardle is using Raven Black.

George Ridgway Killmister and William Challinor, solicitors, are still in partnership at No. 10 Derby Street.

1836 – **Battle of the Alamo**

Leek Total Abstinence Society is formed by Charles Carus Wilson.

A lending library for teachers, pupils and parents is set up at the Sunday school on the site of the Grammar School.

The Primitive Methodist chapel is built at the west end of Fountain Street and a Sunday school is begun.

James Morrow, the minister of the Derby Street Congregational Chapel, and master of the Derby Street Academy, dies. The school continues. On his death, the two congregations are reunited, using the Union Street chapel and retaining the Derby Street chapel for Sunday school and, until 1845, for midweek services.

The Vicar's income is £191 1s. 4d., consisting of £60 14s. in rent from land and sittings and in income from sermons endowments, £50 in Easter dues, £60 in fees, and £20 7s. 4d. in dividends from the 1824 grant.

1837 – Queen Victoria

The Leek Poor Law Union is formed and a new Union Workhouse is built on Ashbourne Road (now the Moorlands Hospital) designed in the classical style by Bateman and Drury of Birmingham. (The compiler's father, when a patient in the hospital, used to say that he "*never thought that he would end his days in the workhouse*".)

Joshua Nicholson joins the firm of Joshua and James Brough and Co. as a "*traveller*" (i.e. a commercial salesman, out "on the road".)

The annual Venison Feast is held early in October with venison supplied by the Duke of Sutherland, the owner of Wall Grange Farm in Longsdon.

Joshua Brough, of the silk manufacturing firm of Joshua and James Brough and Co., builds Buxton Villa on Buxton Road at the junction with Abbotts Road at time of his marriage to the daughter of William Spooner Littlehales of Erdington (then in Warwickshire).

The Quaker women's meeting still exists.

The archdeacon notes that an old font has been moved into the church from the outside.

The Sunday school on the site of the Grammar School has 244 boys and 243 girls on the roll.

The Manor Court appoints a crier.

The Leek Literary and Mechanics' Institute is formed. To be associated with it at various times are Joshua Brough JP, John Brough JP, WS Brough, Edwin Brough and John Ward JP. It is a science and debating society, and a chess club and musical and other courses are run. There is also a circulating library. It meets in rented premises, at first in the school at Derby Street at the Congregational Chapel. It is led by William France, a silk manufacturer, who aims the early publicity at those working men who wish to better themselves. There is a 5s. subscription and 2s. 6d. entry fee, both payable by instalments, and described as "*trifling*".

Richard Cooper is appointed the Medical Officer of the Leekfrith district of Leek Poor Law Union.

The Tithing of Leek manor is apparently known as Lowe.

The Victoria Court of Foresters and Loyal Westwood Lodge of Oddfellows (Manchester Unity) are both formed. They are clubs associated with national friendly societies and combined welfare and socialising. They meet in different inns in the town.

The Manorial Constable is still exercising policing duties,

Water from Hollands Well, adjoining Spout Street, is described as "*pure and excellent*" and is never known to run dry.

The mail coaches cease to run through Leek.

1838 – A ropewalk is situated on the north side of Buxton Road near its junction with Ball Haye Street.

Andrew Jukes Worthington is a partner in Goostrey and Co.

A cricket club is in existence.

Osbourne Street is built.

What is now Ashbourne Road is known as London Road.

The millhands go on strike against a pay cut and the Government Commissioner comes to Leek later in the year.

William Travis, a clockmaker, moves to premises in the Market Place, and remains there until his death.

The Mechanics' Institute has, in October, 145 members. They have a reading room which is open three evenings a week, with a library of almost 500 books, plus pamphlets and periodicals. The first lecture organised by the Institute is delivered in April at the Derby Street chapel.

The road from the canal basin into town, known as Spooner's Lane, is renamed Canal Street.

The silk manufacturers of Leek and its neighbourhood draw up a scheme for a new association for the prosecution of silk thieves.

George Nall, bookseller, stationer and printer in Sheepmarket, is also the postmaster.

The sexton rings the bell at six-acre meadow at 1 p.m. each day.

Messrs Fowler, Haworth and Gaunt occupy part of the premises at the corner of Market Place and Stockwell Street.

Britannia Street is in existence but not yet named.

The stretch of road between the Green Man inn on Compton and Birchall is realigned.

Jukes Worthington marries the niece of Henry Turner's wife.

1839 – At the entrance at the Horton Street Mill, a terrace of ten back-to-back workers' cottages is in existence.

Only half of the 150 broad looms and a third of 180 engine looms are working full time.

The domestic ribbon industry is mainly in the hands of female members of undertakers' families. Journeymen have moved into mills, and apprentices are no longer being taken. Children too are working in the mills.

The Leek PoorLaw Guardians begin a school at the Union Workhouse for the children there and employ a master and mistress.

John Cruso gives up law to devote himself to voluntary work.

By the autumn, various classes are started at the Mechanics' Institute, including one in mutual improvement and another to help members with reading, writing and arithmetic.

The Government Commissioner and John Richards, a Chartist missionary who formed a political union in town, find that many of the millhands are povertystricken and resentful.

John Wreford has fifty looms in his mill in London Street.

The Humane Society (a friendly society) is reorganised as the Leek Independent Male Humane Society.

On a visit to Leek, Wombwell's Menagerie engages a local man, James Bostock of Horton, aged 24. He later marries George Wombwell's niece and takes over the business.

The Leek Philharmonic Society is established by Benjamin Barlow, the organist at St Edward's Church. The Society gives the first in a series of subscription concerts in October in the Assembly Room at The Swan inn.

The Leek Total Abstinence Society is established.

The Leek Wesleyan Sunday School Society is founded.

There are still some forty broadsilk undertakers, with a large number of journeymen. There are no powered broad looms in operation, but some are being erected. Domestic weaving continues to decline.

The Government Commissioners remark on the cleanliness of the town and workers' dwellings.

The workhouse garden is opened in Ashbourne Road.

Many Irish people who formerly worked as broadsilk weavers in Leek have moved to Manchester and Macclesfield and there are now few Irish people in the mills.

Glendinning and Gaunt have ten steampowered looms in the Horton Street Mill, having earlier used Ball Haye Brook to provide power.

Alterations are started to St Edward's Church. They last two years. To the design of John Leech, the nave arcades are rebuilt as three bays where there have previously been four. Jodrell's Chapel is removed and the side galleries are brought forward to the line of arcades. The west end of the north aisle is remodelled to provide a porch with stairs to the west gallery. Besides private subscriptions, grants are received from the Incorporated Church Building Society and the Lichfield Diocesan Church Building Society.

William Challinor dies at 10 Derby Street.

The former Parish Workhouse is put up for sale.

The Moss Rose Lodge of Free Gardeners is founded.

1840 – The Leek Benevolent Burial Society is founded.

At the meetings of the Mechanics' Institute, outside speakers include John Murray, a lecturer on popular science, who gives at least four series of talks at Leek during the decade.

Wesleyans set up a day school in Ball Haye Street and employ a master, trained in the Lancastrian method (?), plus a mistress.

In St Edward's Church, the pulpit is moved to the north side of the chancel arch during alterations.

The Leek branch of The Anti-Corn Law League is formed. (The "Corn Laws" are a series of import duties placed upon corn. The effect is to protect the British producers but to deprive the poor of cheap corn that is available from the corn belt of America.)

The Commercial Bank of England fails.

1841 – Josiah Hastel, a twister, owns a terrace of five houses and a twostoreyed shade in London Street and lives in one of the houses. The upper-floor shade consists of a twisting room and also a winding room where Josiah and his wife employ ten 'piecers' and three 'doublers'. The ground floor is let to four twisters working for whom they wish and employing their own boys.

The lease of the Sheepmarket branch of the Manchester and Liverpool District Bank expires and the Bank reverts to weekly opening in a room in Church Street.

John Cruso, solicitor, dies. His son moves the office from Spout Street to the house in Church Street later known as Foxlowe.

The Pacific Court of Foresters is founded, a Friendly Society.

James Rogers is making rope in Buxton Road.

The Derby Street Academy has closed.

George Ashton is recorded as a watchmaker in Sheepmarket.

The Government Commissioners again remark on the cleanliness of the town and the workers' dwellings. The Commissioner also records a prevalence of fever, which he attributes to "*the neglected state of privies, ditches, boglands, and lanes*". He describes how a silk shade in London Street, itself very dirty, is in a yard behind a row of cottages, each with a privy emptying into the yard. There is only a shallow gutter to carry filth to the cesspool, which is "*equally exposed and of itself enough to poison the whole neighbourhood*".

Distress funds are again established by public subscription for the support of the workhouse.

The Catholic Sunday school has forty pupils.

There is a fourday holiday following the Sunday wake in October and horse racing takes place on the Monday and Tuesday.

Leek's six Sunday schools have 1,607 pupils on their books and an attendance of 80 per cent. There are 168 teachers.

Simeon Rogers is a ropemaker in Well Street.

Samuel Scriven, reporting to the Children's Employment Commission, states that he has found no injury to feet or ankles; on the contrary, boys are healthy and "*notorious for being long winded, and fast runners*".

George Wilkinson sells three farms to John Davenport of Westwood Hall.

"Back of the Street" has been renamed "Belle Vue".

The Wesleyan day school in Ball Haye Street has an average attendance of fifty-four. The children pay sixpence a week for reading, writing and arithmetic, and ninepence a week if they are also taught grammar, history and geography. Girls are offered free instruction in needlework, knitting and marking clothes. (Does this mean labelling? Or is it perhaps a printing error for "making clothes"?) The children's parents are millworkers and tradespeople. The master states that they pay fairly regularly, although fees are higher than in most schools.

1842 – William Michael Hilliard, bookseller, has moved to Market Place.

A friendly society for Anglican men is founded.

The troubles strengthen the feeling that Anglican day schools for workingclass children are needed in town with a salaried master and mistress who teach both day and Sunday schools. The curriculum is to include reading, writing and arithmetic, with some natural history and geography for certain children. Knitting and sewing is for the girls. The fees are to be one penny or threepence a week.

Francis Cruso, the brother of John Cruso, is practising as a solicitor in Stockwell Street.

In January, the Leek branch of the AntiCorn Law League sponsors a petition to the Queen from the women of Leek drawing her attention to workingclass distress in the town.

Benjamin Barlow, the organist at St Edward's Church, arranges for Joseph Mainzer, a pioneer teacher of choirs according to the solfa method, to give lectures in Leek on congregational singing.

Chartist disturbances take place. (The Chartists were members of a political movement calling for an extension of the franchise – the right to vote – to the working classes, so called because supporters signed "The Charter".)

On Saturday 13 August, groups of young men arrive in town. They are strikers from neighbouring manufacturing towns who go around begging at houses. The following day, the Leek magistrates are informed that several thousand men are occupying Congleton and preparing to march on Leek. The magistrates swear in 350 special constables and send to the Potteries for troops. They organise a mounted patrol of the parish. On 15 August, the Newcastle and Pottery troop of yeomanry cavalry arrive. Young men and boys, armed with bludgeons, are drifting into the town from Congleton. The main body of marchers, 2,000 of the 4,000 men, arrive at 11.00 a.m., mainly from Congleton and Macclesfield with a few from Stockport and Manchester. Preceded by a band, they march into Market Place, where they are confronted by the magistrates, the yeomanry and the specials. After a brief altercation, the marchers assure the magistrates that no violence is intended and they are allowed to pass. Some beg for food and money. Others go around the silk mills and dye-works, forcing those not already closed by strike to shut. The marchers then assemble at the cattle market for a meeting. The leaders call on the Leek workers to join the general strike. In the afternoon, most of the marchers return to Congleton. Some remain to organise a march on the Potteries the following day, 16 August. They sleep in a plantation on the Ball Haye estate and are fed by local sympathisers. There are riots in the Potteries on 15 August, and on 16 August the Newcastle and Pottery Yeomanry return from Leek to restore order there. The marchers who have remained at Leek overnight set off for the Potteries accompanied by large number of Leek workers. A troop of dragoons has already been called out to deal with looting in Burslem. The magistrates there receive news of the approach of the Leek and Congleton men and read the Riot Act. (Under the terms of the Act a Magistrate fearing an imminent breach of the peace may read aloud a declaration calling upon the persons assembled to disperse. If they fail to do with within a set period of time, they are deemed to be an Unlawful Assembly and may be dispersed with force.) The marchers arrive and begin to stone the dragoons, who open fire. Several marchers are wounded and Josiah Heapy, a nineteenyearold Leek shoemaker, is killed. The dragoons charge the crowd and disperse it. Later that day, the leading inhabitants of Leek, fearing that the town could be overrun, send urgent appeals for troops. In the evening, large amounts of bread are handed out to the poor. On 17 August, the District Army Commander agrees to send a company of the 34th Regiment of Foot and the Lichfield troop of yeomanry, which are in Newcastle. The Yeomanry reach Leek the same day and the infantry arrive on the 18th. Heapy's funeral is held at St Edward's but there is no disorder. The silk masters and the dyers reopen their works the following morning. The troops are still at Leek on 20 August, but there are no further disturbances.

In September, two Sunday school teachers are disciplined for involvement with the Chartists. Charles Rathbone, the master at St Edward's Sunday school, joined the march from Leek to Burslem. He expresses regret and is suspended for two months without pay. Elizabeth Phillips, the mistress at the school, having declared her support for the Chartists, refuses to express regret and is dismissed.

The Mechanics' Institute pays for new "snuffers" for candles.

"The Staffordshire Regiment of Gentlemen and Yeomanry" and the troop of infantry are revived following the Chartist disturbances earlier in the year. They are styled "The Leek and Moorlands Troop" and later become part of "The Queen's Own Royal Yeomanry".

1843 – No horse races are held in Leek this year.

Leek Friends' preparative meeting is discontinued. They join the meeting in StokeuponTrent. Sunday meetings for worship, however, are still held at Leek.

At the Mechanics' Institute, drawing classes begin.

The Trustees of Town Lands open day schools for boys and girls in the Sunday school on the site of the Grammar School building, to supplement the Sunday school.

George Nall, bookseller, stationer and printer in Sheepmarket, also postmaster, moves his business and post office to Custard Street.

1844 – The Education Act introduces compulsory half-time education for all children

Day schools are united with the National Society and are established in the town to supplement or replace the system of secular instruction offered at the Sunday schools.

The Cricket Club is reorganised as the "Leek and Moorlands Cricket Club". They play at Barnfields. The Club holds a meeting at the Town Hall on 20 May.

A second gas holder is built at the gasworks.

Brough's Mill

Boys at the Union Workhouse school are taught knitting and straw plaiting.

Another Wesleyan Methodist Sunday school opens in Ball Haye Street. There are still over 400 pupils at the West Street School.

Joshua and James Brough and Co. build a new factory in Union Street.

1845 – The district of St Luke is formed out of St Edward's parish. It covers the eastern part of the Leek and Lowe township, including most of the eastern side of Leek town, and also the Tittesworth township. The patronage of a perpetual curacy is vested in the Crown and the Bishop alternately, with the Crown making first presentation. Benjamin Pidcock is the first minister (1845/82). At first, he holds services in a room over a stable in the yard of the Black's Head inn in Derby Street. The Ecclesiastical Commissioners agree to pay the minister £100 year, with a further £30 when the building is licensed for worship and a total of £150 on the consecration of the church.

A building between Prince Street and Pump Street opens as a Methodist Sunday school.

Jukes Worthington buys out Turners and the firm becomes A.J. Worthington and Co.

An infants' school is opened at the Wesleyans' day school in Ball Haye Street. It proves to be too ambitious and too expensive and soon closes.

A Roman Catholic day school is opened. The schoolhouse is built behind the Roman Catholic chapel for a day school with separate rooms for boys and girls. The children are taught together since there is hardly enough money to pay for one teacher. A Roman Catholic priest commented: *"No books. No maps. No desks."*

The Congregationalists of Union Street Chapel build a twostoreyed Sunday school next to the chapel.

The Rising Sun Lodge of Druids is founded.

1846 – Potato famine in Ireland

Methodist Services begin again at Ball Haye Green when the Ball Haye Green chapel opens, with a Sunday school.

B.B. Nixon starts working for Joshua and James Brough and Co. just before his sixteenth birthday.

"The Pride of the Moorlands Lodge of the Order of Sisters" is formed. It is a friendly society for Anglican women.

The Leek and North Staffordshire Benefit Building and Investment Society is formed, but the venture is unsuccessful.

With grants from society and government, the Trustees of Town Lands buy three cottages and land adjoining the schoolhouse on site of the Grammar School. The cottages are for the teachers' houses and part of the land is for a playground.

The gas undertaking is sold to the Improvement Commissioners and the company is dissolved.

The Quaker Sunday meetings are discontinued.

The first Friday in August is the customary day for friendly societies to parade. The date is probably chosen to coincide with Stoke Wakes. The event attracts many people who come from the Potteries by canal boat. The lodges of national friendly societies also take part in the friendly societies parade.

The land bounded by Queen Street and Fountain Street is bought as a site for a church and school.

The Congregationalists of Union Street open a day school for infants, which they claim to be the first in Leek. They appoint a mistress from the Infant School Society.

The Leek branch of the Anti-Corn Law League is disbanded.

1847 – Factory Act – women and children aged thirteen to eighteen to work no more than ten hours per day

A County Court district is established.

The Bank of Fowler, Haworth and Gaunt, consisting of Sarah Fowler of Horton Hall, John Haworth of Cliffe Park in Horton, and John and Matthew Gaunt, Sarah's sons by her first marriage, closes.

The Congregationalists' Infants School in Union Street has an attendance of fifty, aged two to six. The children pay a few pence, but the school is financed chiefly by donations and subscriptions.

John Brough dies.

Samuel Tatton has built Hencroft.

John Cruso lays the foundation stone of St Luke's Church.

There is an average attendance at Sunday school on the site of the Grammar School of 343.

The Church Sunday school ceases to teach writing; instead the master and two helpers give writing lessons free on Friday evenings. The numbers attending Sunday school then decline because writing is no longer taught.

Day and Sunday schools for St Luke's district are built in Fountain Street. Services are held in the building until the opening of St Luke's Church. The promoters intend that the day school, initially for infants only, should admit older children if there is sufficient demand. The school is financed by subscriptions, donations and the children's pence.

The Mechanics' Institute join the Midlands Union of Literary and Mechanics' Institutions.

St Luke's Church school is opened and services are transferred there.

The average attendance at the day school on the site of the Grammar School is 126.

A plan to replace the Town Hall in the Market Place with a grander building on another site in the Market Place comes to nothing.

1848 – On 27 July round-arm bowling is introduced in a cricket match against Cheadle.

A County Police Station is built at the junction of Mill Street and West Street, including a dwelling for an inspector and three cells in place of the two in the Town Hall. The police station includes a court room where the Petty Sessions are held.

Roebuck Lane is renamed Russell Street.

The Mechanics' Institute moves to larger rooms at the chapel.

St Luke's Church is consecrated. It consists of a chancel with a north vestry and a north organ chamber, an aisled nave of five bays with south porch, and a west tower with a southeast turret. Built of sandstone in Gothic style, it is designed by

F.J. Francis of London. The tower has not been built beyond the first stage. The cost is met by subscriptions and grants from the Lichfield Diocesan Church Extension Society, the Incorporated Church Building Society and Sir Robert Peel's Fund. Money is also raised by the sale of land on Ashbourne Road left by Sarah Brentnall, née Grosvenor, as a site for a church.

John Davenport dies at Westwood. His son John greatly enlarges the estate by buying the neighbouring farms.

Land is rented by the Union Workhouse school near the Workhouse and the children are taught spade cultivation.

Leek Operative Floral Society exists.

Cornhill Street and Jolliffe Street are described as intended new streets.

1849 – A friendly society for members of the Congregational church is founded.

On 17 September, a meeting is held at the George and a committee of five is formed to organise horse racing in Leek.

Over ten acres of land has been lost by the Trustees of Town Lands, mainly through their failure to collect rents. The thirty-four acres remaining produces rents of £90 19s.

James Wardle, the Leek silk manufacturer, gives a house in Regent Street as a Methodist manse.

The Mechanics' Institute has 226 members, and the library, open six nights a week, has grown to 1,250 volumes. The range of instruction has been broadened.

William Sugden comes to Leek as the architect and surveyor of the Churnet Valley railway line. He is from Keighley, Yorkshire and he is to supervise the stations being built on the railway.

The plant nursery of William Nunns is at Barngates, where plants, rhubarb and cabbages are stolen from it.

The Guardians of the Leek PoorLaw Union appoint an Inspector of Nuisances, to inspect the town and report any nuisances to them.

The Churnet Valley railway opens with a station on Newcastle Road.

Leek Original Floral and Horticultural Society Annual Show is held at the Blue Ball Inn in Mill Street.

Because the railway has arrived, omnibuses are introduced from the Red Lion and the Roebuck to the station on Newcastle road.

Complaints are made are about the water supply. The springs near Wall Grange, in Longsdon, provide a good supply to the Potteries, but Leek's supply is both inadequate and impure. The inhabitants are constantly annoyed by the bellman's calling out, *"The water will be turned off all day tomorrow"* and *"The reservoir and fountain are full of fish, frogs, toads, tadpoles etc."*

Complaints are also made that the main sewers are too small to carry away all of the sewage of the town.

The Railway comes to Rudyard.

William Sugden sets up on his own account.

The managers of St Luke's School allow the master to run his own school for boys, in a room in the building.

1850 – There is a commercial newsroom in Stockwell Street.

The former French POW, Alexandre Gay, dies aged 65. He married the daughter of Thomas Beard of Ball Haye Road.

Number 8 Stockwell Street is the cardboard box factory of James Brough, who also owns number 10, later the Fire Station.

Larner Sugden is born in Leek.

The old Black's Head is demolished. A New Black's Head is to be built, designed by Sugden.

George Nall, printer and bookseller, runs a subscription library and a public circulating library.

Alfred Overfield is trading as an upholsterer and cabinet maker in Sheepmarket.

Two terminating societies are launched within few days of each other. (A terminating society is one that is brought into being for a specific purpose, e.g. to build twelve houses for members, and which terminates once that objective has been achieved). These are the Leek United Benefit Building Society and the Leek Benefit Building Society.

The Railway Company takes over a house near the station and opens it as the Churnet Valley Hotel.

The Nab Hill tunnel through the high ground to the north is built to resemble a natural cavern in rock, with no masonry at either entrance.

A stone structure has been erected at Ladydale Well.

There is also a May Day procession to the site by the children from St Mary's Roman Catholic Church.

The Grosvenor family own the 65-acre Moorhouse Farm.

James Rogers has moved his ropewalk to Spout Street.

There are five cabinet makers in town.

The annual procession of Sunday school children is held. It is known as Cap Sunday from the caps worn by the girls.

Leek and Lowe has its own vestry meeting.

Horse races are still taking place at Birchall Dale.

About this time there are usually about half a dozen private schools in the town.

The Mechanics' Institute has over sixty pupils attending classes. Subjects included singing, chemistry and French.

A Penny Bank (one specifically designed to encourage small sums to be deposited) is set up at the Institute for 295 members and for townspeople in general.

William Michael Hilliard, bookseller, has moved to Sheepmarket.

The fair held on 3 July has dwindled to being a fair for the sale of scythes only.

A dyeing mill has been established at the junction of Mill Street and Abbey Green Road, using the water of the River Churnet.

Albert Street is created when thirteen building plots there are offered for sale.

The Saturday market is dealing chiefly in meat and vegetables.

A shade is added on the Union Street site.

The mill in West Street becomes the Britannia Mill after a partial rebuilding.

Mary Elizabeth, the wife of John Cruso junior, dies.

1851 – Ralph Mountfort and Son is described as a firm of grocers and rope and twine spinners.

The Cock Low is described as being 40 yards in diameter and 18 feet high. An excavation uncovers a flint implement and fragments of an urn and of human bone.

A County Court is held monthly at the Red Lion.

A Horticultural Society exists.

Britannia Street, which has been in existence since 1838, is named.

John Davenport, the younger, makes further extensions to Westwood Hall, designed by Weightman, Hadfield and Goldie of Sheffield and including a great hall and a tower at the west end of the south front and extensive buildings around the courtyard on the northwest extensions, which are in stone on principal elevations and dark red brick elsewhere, in a plain Elizabethan style, and surviving elevations by Elmes are altered to conform to it. Improvements to the grounds have been made by John Davenport the elder and included a terraced lawn to the east of the house with an ornamental retaining wall, entrance gates to the southeast, and a Gothic outbuilding with a tower and a spire to the southwest. Further southwest are early 19thcentury stables, which are used as farm buildings after coach houses and stables are built west of house.

The first house in Westwood Terrace, linking West Street and Britannia Street, is built.

Samuel Phillips, a silk manufacturer with a mill at Barngates, dies.

Leek has three silk-dyeing firms'

Four gardeners in town include William Nunns, who landscaped the ground on the west side of Rudyard Lake.

Land between Belle Vue, West Street and the southern end of Garden Street is laid out as twenty-four building plots.

On Census Sunday, there is a total of 1,049 Sunday school children who attend the town's churches and chapels (523 Wesleyan Methodists, 336 Anglicans, 90 Congregationalists, 51 Primitive Methodists and 49 Roman Catholics). In the afternoon 791 children attend; Wesleyan Methodists (404) and Anglicans (278) predominate.

The Primitive Methodist chapel at the west end of Fountain Street has a congregation of 59 in morning, besides Sunday school children, and 217 in the evening.

The Roman Catholic congregation numbers 167 in morning and 115 in the evening, besides Sunday school children.

Adult attendances are 1,510 at the Wesleyan Methodist chapels, 276 at the Primitive

Methodist chapel and 288 at the Congregational chapel, In contrast, 1,293 attend at the two Anglican churches and 282 at the Roman Catholic church.

The Union Street chapel has congregations of 120 in the morning, besides Sunday school children, and 168 in the evening.

There are congregations of 294 at Mount Pleasant Methodist, 124 at Brunswick, afternoon congregations of 161 at Mount Pleasant and 60 at Ball Haye Green, and evening congregations of 517 at Mount Pleasant, 296 at Brunswick, and 58 at Ball Haye Green. There are also Sunday schools at all three places.

The two schools of St Luke's have an average attendance of 150.

Attendance at St Luke's is 83 in morning and 110 in afternoon, besides Sunday school children.

The managers of St Luke's School give the master notice to quit.

A Health Scheme is instituted. Adults pay one penny a week and children a halfpenny. Four surgeons are available. Honorary subscribers pay 21 shillings a year, for which they could recommend five or six patients. Midwifery cases are counted as two ordinary cases.

The Leek County Police Force consists of a Superintendent, an Inspector, and eleven men.

The average attendance at the day school on the site of the Grammar School is 141.

The average attendance at the Sunday school opened on the site of the Grammar School is 257.

The owner refuses permission for the use of the course and the horse races are cancelled.

After horse racing is stopped, many people go instead on the Monday to Trentham Gardens, Belle Vue in Manchester or other attractions.

Samuel Travis, son of William Travis, has his own business as a clock and watchmaker in Market Place It continues there until the early 1880s.

Alfred Overfield is in business in Queen Street as a furniture broker and cabinetmaker.

A new Cricket Club is formed in Leek, the "Leek Albion".

There are two brickmakers in London Road.

A Racing Committee meets at the King William IV in Church Street to inspect a proposed new course at Leek Edge.

Fees and Easter offerings bring in a further £30 at St Luke's Church.

John Ashton aged 75 is still working as a clockmaker in Sheepmarket.

A brewer named Ralph Tatton is living in Stockwell Street. He is not known to have traded in Leek.

John Cruso is appointed the Manor Steward of Leek. He marries his second wife, Anne Searight, who is 21 years younger than he.

A girls' school kept by the Mellor family exists. It is to be the longestlived 19th century school and survives until the 1890s.

1852 – Free use of the ground in Beggars Lane is given by John Davenport to the Leek and Moorlands Cricket Club.

The reservoirs are enlarged.

The Lodge to Westwood Hall is built on the eastern drive.

Alsop Street is laid out over land belonging to James Alsop, the promoter of the Leek Benefit Building Society.

A brick sewer is constructed from Market Place down Spout Street (later St Edward Street) and Canal Street to discharge into a ditch.

1853 – On 28 October, an indenture is drawn up between Isambard Kingdom Brunel and James Michael Holdship of the first part and John Cruso of the second part and Joshua Brough, Thomas Birch, Robert Hammersley and John Brough of the third part (all are Building Society Directors).

Mount Pleasant Methodist Chapel is enlarged and a new organ fitted.

Ball Haye Hall is sold by Court Order plus 42 acres, for £5,150 to J. and J. Brough.

James Bostock marries the niece of his boss, Mr Wombwell of the Travelling Menagerie.

The Leek Silk Twisters' Friendly Society is in existence. It is the only benefit society known to have been associated with trade.

The Leek and Moorlands Provident Association (a friendly society) is founded.

The managers of St Luke's open their own boys' school in the room which the master has vacated. The schools then begin to receive a government grant. The new master, Joseph Sykes, enrols some middleclass boys, who are charged higher fees and for an additional payment taught subjects such as Latin and algebra. Sykes also takes boarders, at one point jeopardising the school's grant by not following government regulations.

Wellington Mills in Strangman's Walk, later Strangman Street, are built.

The boys' and girls' day schools on the site of the Grammar School are merged and an infants' school is established in what has been the boys' schoolroom, beginning with sixty-seven children.

At Ball Haye Green, Nelson Street is laid out on part of the Ball Haye estate.

London Mill on the corner of Ashbourne Road (formerly London Road) and Well Street is built.

Samuel Tatton opens his second works.

John Snape's Travelling Theatre plays at Leek during Wakes Week.

The Prince Albert Lodge of Oddfellows is founded.

The trustees of Leek Savings Bank begin building on the corner of Derby Street and Russell Street to a design of William Sugden.

The upper room of the old Town Hall, at the bottom of Market Square, ceases being used.

1854 – James Brough dies.

The public baths, designed in an Elizabethan style by F. and W. Francis of London, are opened at the east end of Derby Street.

W.B. Badnall becomes the soninlaw of Francis Cruso, and takes over most of the Cruso practice.

The Mechanics' Institute moves from Derby Street to premises in Russell Street. Following several years of quarrels over the management, some of the stricter Nonconformist members object to the proposal to buy novels for the library and try to ban chess and draughts. It is alleged that Sunday opening is being contemplated. Their opponents accuse them of Calvinistic intolerance. It is stated that many of the library books are unread because they are too abstruse for the Mechanics' Institute, and it is claimed that much of the Institute's educational effort has been of little use to "*the poor working boy*". They urge that future presidents should be men with a real interest in the Institute and not merely local notables. The Institute moves away from the chapel precincts, but there is no schism. The Mechanics' Institute retains a strong Nonconformist character.

Alfred Overfield, the cabinetmaker, moves to Russell Street.

Park Road running from Ball Haye Road to Abbey Green Road across the Ball Haye estate is built.

Mark Abbott, a ropemaker, lives at an address in Buxton Road.

There are two brewers in town: Thomas Clowes, who keeps the Pump Inn in Mill Street, and George Walker, who has a brewery at the junction of Canal Street (later Broad Street) and Alsop Street.

Derby Street

St Luke's Church is completed to the specifications of F.J. Francis and his brother Horace. At same time a wall is built around the churchyard.

The Leek Horticultural Society is reformed as the Leek Floral and Horticultural Society.

William Michael Hillard, the bookseller of Sheepmarket, has added auctioneering to his business.

Wellington Street linking Britannia Street and Strangman's Walk is built, when four newly erected houses there are advertised for sale.

Silk is being made in greater lengths and also involves spooling.

John Davenport is appointed sheriff.

Attendance at the Sunday school on the site of the Grammar school is still falling.

Joseph Sykes of St Luke's School successfully demands a pay rise.

The Union Workhouse school employs a master and a mistress.

The Wesleyans' Sunday school in West Street is rebuilt on a larger scale. It is redesigned by William Sugden.

The West Street School opens as a day school.

1855   **The first iron Cunard steamer crosses Atlantic**

Florence Nightingale is in the Crimea

Several silk manufacturers have their premises in Compton.

In December, the Commissioners transfer their meetings from the public hall in the Market Place to a room in Derby Street.

The new Black's Head public house is built, designed by Sugden.

Houses are built at the junction of Abbotts Road and Novi Lane.

Market Street, Silk Street, York Street and Deansgate are laid out.

Reading and writing are still taught at the West Street Sunday school.

E.F.T. Ribbans, the master of the Leek Grammar School, is also the curate at St Edward's and the chaplain of the workhouse.

A mixed day school is opened in the Wesleyans' Sunday school in West Street.

West Street day school has forty pupils, who pay three or fourpence per week. The fourpenny pupils are taught grammar besides reading, writing and arithmetic. The school receives a government grant.

Brunswick Street is built.

Eleven cottages making up Inkerman Terrace are built.

The right to the fair and market tolls is owned by William Grosvenor's widow Mary, Edward Rooke and the trustee of Grosvenor's will.

The Canal Road tollhouse is out of use and is replaced by one near Wallbridge.

A newly erected shade in Duke Street is advertised for sale. It consists of four storeys, with a second floor used as a warehouse and a winding room.

Leek Cricket Club has its first professional player, J. Copson. He is paid one shilling per match.

At the Manchester and Liverpool District Bank, daily opening is resumed in the premises in Custard Street.

A pleasure fair forms part of the May fair.

A reservoir is built at Blackshaw Moor, from which water is piped to the other two.

The Earl of Macclesfield's yearly income from water supply is £586 and expenditure on repairs and maintenance is estimated at between £60 and £70.

A new body of twenty-four Improvement Commissioners is established with wider powers than its predecessor under an Act of Parliament, with responsibility for an area within a 1,500-yard radius from the gas lamp in the centre of Market Place. Stones marking the boundary are erected on all main roads and elsewhere, and several survive.

One of the aims of the 1855 Improvement Act is that the new Commissioners should take over the water supply.

1856 – The Leek and Moorland Building Society is established on a permanent basis at 15 Stockwell Street with an office at 1 Stockwell Street and with upwards of 120 members.

The Wesleyan Sunday school in West Street stops teaching reading and writing.

Leek Total Abstinence Society has a lecture room in Stockwell Street.

The quality of the water is good but the reservoirs are in a filthy state, such that "*the water is charged with vegetable matter and very unpure.*" The needs of the town are estimated at an average of 90,000 gallons per day, but the supply is at the rate of "*only 2½ gallons per head per diem for whole population*". Of the 2,117 houses within the Improvement Commissioners' district 1,263 pay a water rate. The main areas wholly or partially without a supply are the lower part of Mill Street, Belle Vue, Kiln Lane, Leek Moor and Ball Haye Green, and many people depend on the polluted water from wells and the River Churnet.

The Commissioners buy the waterworks for £11,000.

Weston Street exists, taking its name from the owner of the land.

Duke Street and South Street exist.

Eight building plots in Westwood Terrace are advertised as "*eligible sites for a better class of houses*".

The Commissioners' Waterworks Committee states that the income could be doubled if the powers given by the 1827 Act are fully used.

"*Great mortality*" in the town leads the Improvement Commissioners to set up a medical committee to report on local conditions.

A surpliced choir exists at St Luke's Church.

Land on the Ball Haye estate is bought as a site for a house for the vicar of St Luke's Church.

The Improvement Commissioners, who are already paying the cost of the lighting of St Edward's Church clock, agree to pay the cost of repairing and attending it also.

The timber ceiling of the nave of St Edward's Church is restored by Ewan Christian.

The chancel of St Edward's Church is rebuilt to a design of G.E. Street. A south aisle, with an arcade of two bays, is added for an organ and extra seating. At same time the base of the tower, which has been walled off from the nave and used as a mason's workshop, is opened into the nave.

Victoria Street is built.

Joshua and John Brough enter into partnership with Joshua Nicholson and B.B. Nixon.

The two bodies of Congregationalists are reunited and their own church is erected on the site of the chapel. It is designed by Sugden.

The Society of New Connexion Methodists is formed in Leek, meeting first in the Temperance Society's lecture room in Stockwell Street and then in the Friends' meeting house at Overton Bank.

From Ann Jolliffe's charity (see 1732) the Cornhill Cross land is sold to the Improvement Commissioners to form part of the new cemetery.

The surveyor urges the adoption of water closets throughout the town.

Joseph Sykes of St Luke's School successfully demands another pay rise.

1857 – The Medical Committee report on local conditions is published. It notes "*the vicious and intemperate habits of people*", inadequate ventilation in the factories, bad drainage and an insufficient water supply. The Canal Street (later Broad Street) area is particularly insanitary, and there is an inadequate provision of privies to be found in "*Beard's houses*" in Compton, where there is only one privy for ten houses. Another group of houses in Compton, known as O'Donnell's Square, is described as "*a system of building outrageous to the sense of the 19th century*". Ball Haye Brook has become an open sewer, and the report adds that in no other town of similar size is "*filth and ordure more liberally bestowed.*" A system of arterial sewers is recommended, as is the appointment of a Medical Officer of Health.

The Leek Philharmonic Society still exists.

The graveyard at Mount Pleasant is closed for burials.

Brunswick Chapel in Regent Street is replaced by the chapel of the same name in Market Street. Built of brick with stone dressings, it is designed in a Gothic style by William Sugden and paid for by James Wardle.

Junction Road is laid out by John Davenport of Westwood Hall across the Barnfields farm to link the Cheddleton and Newcastle roads.

The Leek United Choral Society is in existence, a Nonconformist group.

Big Mill is completed in Mill Street, designed by William Sugden.

The cemetery is opened at Cornhill Cross.

Rose Bank House in Rose Bank Street is designed by William Sugden.

Angle Street is built but not so named until 1867.

Milk Street, Prince Street and Pump Street (built previously) are named.

The ropewalk off Abbotts Road is being worked by Mark Abbott.

The cemetery contractors are given permission to get stone in Thomas Sneyd's quarries in Ballington Wood.

The new cemetery is opened by the Improvement Commissioners on 5½ acres on the west side of Cheddleton Road at Cornhill Cross for the inhabitants of Leek and Lowe, Tittesworth, Rudyard and Longsdon. Nearly 2½ acres are consecrated as Church of England burial ground, and another part is set aside for Roman Catholics. Two mortuary chapels, linked by an archway surmounted by tower and spire, are designed by William Sugden. St. Edward's Church and churchyard is closed for new burials, as are the graveyards attached to Mount Pleasant Wesleyan Methodist Chapel and Derby Street Congregationalist Chapel.

The Sexton is still being paid five shillings for ringing the curfew bell.

Mountfords own a ropewalk then in operation at Ball Haye Green.

There is a drum and fife band in Leek.

Benjamin Barlow, the organist at St Edward's Church, founds the Leek Church Choral Society.

The Highfield Moss Rose Lodge of Free Gardeners is founded.

A organ is installed in Brunswick Methodist Chapel.

A new house for the vicar of St Luke's Church is built.

The town's Temperance Society plans to build a public hall.

A bank is opened by F.W. Jennings in a house at No. 7 Stockwell Street enlarged for the purpose to the design of William Sugden.

Big Mill

The New Connexion Methodists form the Sunday school.

The Cornhill site is acquired for the chapels for the new cemetery.

Charles Slagg is a surveyor.

The Leek Improvement Commissioners' Medical Committee deplore the fact that the dispensary's annual income does not exceed £10 and urges a greater publicising of its work.

William Challinor complains of Leek's notoriety compared with "*places less favoured by nature and circumstances but more by sanitary improvement*."

The Moorlands Lodge of Oddfellows is founded.

Number 1 Stockwell Street is a low stone building and it is enlarged by Sugden for J.W. Jennings, bookkeeper and broker.

1858 – The Annual Town Ball is held at the Red Lion.

The Leek branch of the YMCA is established.

The Mechanics' Institute is generally known as the "Literary and Mechanics' Institute".

Joseph Sykes of St Luke's School engages the school's first pupil teacher, William Beresford, who later becomes the vicar of St Luke's.

The town is divided into two drainage districts, the South and the North, with the sewerage of the South district discharging into the Birchall meadows.

Big Mill in Mill Street is occupied by Joseph Broster. It is six storeys high, twenty-one bays long and five bays deep.

A problem is created for the dye-works by the muddying of the Churnet when Staffordshire Potteries Water Works Co. completes Tittesworth reservoir. Some firms switch to water supplied by the Improvement Commissioners.

1859 – Charles Darwin publishes *On the Origin of Species*

Club Day is transferred from its traditional date of the first Sunday in September and the girls stop wearing the caps.

The Horticultural Society is known as the Leek Original Floral and Horticultural Society.

The Medical Officer of Health is appointed by the Commissioners because of the high rate of mortality in the town.

A drinking fountain is erected on Buxton Road south of its junction with Mount Road by Joshua Brough. It is designed by William Sugden. It incorporates a spring which has long been used by the public, and is intended for the refreshment of the many people who stroll out to the area in summer.

The company of rifle volunteers is formed.

A Swedenborgian missionary from Manchester gives lectures in Leek, but no society is formed.

The Commissioners extend the water main to Ball Haye Green, considered to be the unhealthiest part of town.

Joseph Challinor goes into partnership with William Beaumont Badnall.

Although all 650 sittings are free at St Luke's Church, a voluntary payment is made for some until 1859 when a weekly offertory is introduced instead.

Henry Sneyd dies. He is the incumbent of Wetley Rocks who promoted the plan for a church in the Compton area, with a school and a house for the incumbent. By his death, the site has been acquired in Compton, but there is not enough money for the full scheme to be implemented.

The infants' school in the Wesleyans school in Ball Haye Street has an average attendance of ninety. The evening school is run by the organisers of the infants' school and is held three nights a week.

The Royal Victoria Lodge of Oddfellows is founded.

The South section sewage drainage system is completed.

Workmen digging in Birchall meadows west of the Cheddleton road break into a mound where a cinerary urn (one containing cremated ashes and bones) is discovered.

Because the crowds of onlookers who are attracted to the event are considered to be inappropriate for a Sunday, the Childrens' Sunday school procession is moved to the afternoon of Club Day, the first Friday in August. The children walk with banners and flags and are accompanied by bands.

The rights to the fair and market tolls are bought from Mrs Grosvenor and Edward Rooke by the Leek Improvement Commissioners.

Miles Simpson moves his factory from Middleton, Lancashire, bringing with him some of his workers involved in the Co-op movement. A small cottage on Clerk Bank, owned by a tailor named Armitt, is rented and the shop opened. It is known as the Leek and Moorlands Industrial Provident Society.

1860 – Robert, the son of George Nall, printer, joins the firm, later to be George Nall and Son.

Thomas Clowes, brewer, has gone out of business.

Simeon Rogers has moved his ropewalk to Queen Street.

The friendly societies' parade is known as Club Day.

A drum and fife band is formed by the recently established rifle volunteers.

In the last ten years, three lodges of Oddfellows have been formed, belonging to the Grand United Order.

Joseph Sykes, the master of St Lukes National school, resigns and opens a commercial school at Ball Haye Hall.

The Mechanics' Institute has 287 members "*of all classes*".

E.F.T. Ribbans, the master of Leek Grammar School, leaves Leek after well-publicised accusations that he has fathered an illegitimate child. His successor, P.N. Lawrence, is also the workhouse chaplain and the perpetual curate at St Luke's.

The number of private schools has dwindled. They were usually the middleclass schools, and generally for older children.

Leek Art School is formed.

The Manchester and Liverpool District Bank moves to Derby Street.

The Leek and Moorlands Co-operative Society moves shop to Overton Bank.

William Condlyffe is still practising as a solicitor.

William Challinor is living at Pickwood; Joseph Challinor at 10 Derby Street; and W.B. Badnall in Church Lane.

Joseph Anderson, the Roman Catholic priest, establishes a small community of Irish nuns in the presbytery, and he himself goes to live in lodgings. The nuns are members of the Institute of the Blessed Virgin Mary, and they take over the running of St Mary's School and its fifty pupils from the girl who has been running it. They also start an evening school and open a private school with seventeen children.

For the first time, the children from Church of England Sunday schools take part in Club Day. They walk on their own, after the Wesleyans have finished singing in the Market Place.

Woodhead and Carter, iron and brass founders, millwrights and engineers, have works near the railway station.

The Union Street chapel decide to build a larger chapel on the Derby Street site.

The fire engine house is on the open space at the end of Derby Street. The commissioners are exercising their power to ban the use of thatch as a roofing material.

The death rate in Leek is thirty per 1,000 per annum.

Charles Flint, a local surgeon, gives a drinking fountain, built into the wall of the Town Hall in the Market Place, designed by Sugden.

The disused canal tollhouse is demolished for road widening.

Two ancillary trades have emerged in the town: the manufacture of bobbins and of cardboard boxes.

A night school starts on the site of the Grammar School.

Flint gives a second fountain, set in the wall of the churchyard at the west end of Church Street and fed by the spring.

The infants' school in Ball Haye Street receives a government grant.

On 24 April, Leek Co-op enrols with the Registry of Friendly Societies. Jonathon Grinrod is the first president. The shop is open only evenings and Saturday afternoons.

There is a further expansion between Buxton Road and London Road, and more building and an extension of the silk mills between Fountain Street and London Road by J. and J. Brough, Nicholson and Co.

The silkdyeing industry is expanding.

Jabez Pickford is producing plain and ornamented boxes in Derby Street.

1861 – Beginning of the American Civil War

A survey reveals that there are large numbers of young children employed in the Leek silk industry, many of them working at home or in other places not subject to factory inspection.

The vicarage is enlarged again by G.E. Deacon soon after his institution.

John Cruso is appointed as a director of the District Bank.

There are ten households in Westwood Terrace.

Jukes Worthington is living in Spout Street and his factory employs 200 people.

An evening school is being held at St Luke's School, Fountain Street.

The subbranch of the Manchester and Liverpool District Bank becomes the main branch.

There are three brickmakers in London Road.

A third cricket club is formed in Leek, the "Local Volunteers Company".

Queen Anne's Bounty (see 1793) makes a grant of £150 to meet the benefaction of £300 from the Earl of Macclesfield.

There is a brewery attached to the Blue Ball in Mill Street.

During the trade depression, the Improvement Commissioners provide work for the unemployed, quarrying road stone in Ballington Wood.

The turning of wooden bobbins has become a full-time craft.

The Leek Benefit Building Society is terminated more than two years before its estimated term, having built Alsop Street, Westwood Terrace and St George's Row.

1862 – The Leek Co-op moves to a larger shop just over the road on Overton Bank.

The building on the site of the Grammar School is enlarged.

The sewage drainage system of the north district, discharging at the bottom of Mill Street, is completed. The sewage is distributed over large tracts of land and purified by broad irrigation before passing into the River Churnet.

The Commissioners move to rented premises in Russell Street.

With W.B. Badnall's withdrawal from the practice, the firm of solicitors becomes "Challinor and Challinor".

The New Connexion Methodists chapel, designed by Robert Scrivener of Hanley, opens at the corner of Ball Haye Street and Queen Street.

John Davenport dies. His heir is his son, George.

George Ashton is a watch and clockmaker.

There is another lodge at the entrance to the southern drive to Westwood Hall on Newcastle road near Wallbridge. Both lodges survive as houses.

The Mechanics Institute moves to new premises in Russell Street, costing £869. The three-storeyed building is designed in an Italian style by William Sugden.

St Luke's Church is closed for new burials.

Only one friendly society parades on Club Day, the others finding the cost too great.

The partners in the Commercial Bank are reduced to the elder Badnall and Ellis.

1863 – Separate boys' and girls' schools on the site of the Grammar School are again formed.

The Union Street chapel opens a new chapel, built of stone, in a Decorated style, with a tower and spire, designed by William Sugden, a member of the congregation, on the site of the former homes and chapel. The organ occupies an apse at the south end of the north gallery.

Grammar School

Two bells are added at St Edward's Church, cast by John Warner and Sons of London.

The Roman Catholic Nuns move into a house in King Street, Later the same year, Father Anderson moves into an adjoining cottage owned by Mr Henry Bermingham, who gave the garden as site for the new church, St Mary's.

The Union Workhouse school no longer employs a master, only a mistress

Races are again held on the Birchall Dale course.

The Leek United Permanent Benefit Building Society is formed with premises in Russell Street.

St Edward's Masonic Lodge is formed.

Even in mills using steam power, twisting is still carried out by hand, with only the winding engines being powered.

A brick school/church, designed in the Gothic style by Robert Edgar, opens on the Compton. Variously known as the Compton School Church and Christ Church, it is placed in the charge of an assistant curate at St Luke's.

The main products of the town are coat bindings and sleeve facings.

Estimates of the distance run by the twisters' "trotter", barefoot, in the course of a day's work of ten hours vary from over sixteen miles to nearly twenty. One twister commented that the boy who helped him, aged ten, *"was very tired always at end of his day's work of ten hours"*.

Moorhouse Street is built.

The Leek and Moorlands Permanent Benefit Building Society offers forty-four building lots for sale in two new streets and also in Derby Street and Stockwell Street, which has been widened and raised to improve access; and also in Market Street.

Ford Street and Bath Street are completed. Ford Street is named after Hugh Ford (d. 1830), who had owned the land, and Bath Street takes its name from the baths.

J. and J. Brough, Nicholson and Co. moves to London Mill in Ashbourne Road.

The stall barn, in Derby Street, where the market stalls were kept, is offered for sale.

There are about 300 outtwisters, each employing on average five people, of whom three are aged between nine and sixteen.

The four-day school at St Luke's School, Fountain Street has an average attendance of 200.

Joseph Sykes moves his school to Stockwell Street.

John Kipling meets his future wife at a picnic at Rudyard.

1864 – St Mary's Church is a building of brick and stone designed in the Gothic style by William Sugden. When the church opens, the chapel and house in Fountain Street are sold, the chapel becoming a silk shade.

The Friends' Meeting House at Overton Bank is let to the Christian Brethren, also known as the Plymouth Brethren.

Having bought land at Blackshaw Moor, the Commissioners build a second reservoir there.

The Magistrates' Courts are held in part of the nearby West Street Wesleyan school and continue there until 1879.

When the church is opened in King Street and the Fountain Street building sold, day and private schools are taught in various parts of the new church.

The Leek Economic Loan Society is established with the office in Silk Street, Ball Haye Green.

Thomas Whittles Ltd operate from Wellington Mills in Strangman Street.

John Byrne, a house decorator, has established the North Staffordshire Soda Water Works in Derby Street.

Charles Flint dies at the age of 74, having practised in Leek for nearly fifty years.

Francis Cruso, lawyer, dies.

Leek Total Abstinence Society buys the former Congregational Chapel in Union Street, converts it and opens it as a Temperance Hall.

Leek and Moorlands Subscription Library is run by George Nall's son Robert.

The Bridge End brewery, on the Leekfrith side of the River Churnet, is worked by Dixon and Johnson.

Three fields to the southwest of Westwood Hall, and then part of Wallbridge Farm, are called Rabbit Burrow.

Much of the plateau on which Westwood Hall stands and the adjacent slopes are landscaped with a mixture of small woods and fields.

The east part of St Mary's Church is opened, with the main approach from Compton. It is designed in the Gothic style by Albert Vicars of London and is built of Bath stone. It consists of a chancel with side chapels, an aisled nave of five bays with an organ gallery at the west end, and the lofty southeast tower and spire. There are sacristies in the southeast corner, and the northeast corner is occupied by the former nuns' chapel. The site has been presented by J.H. Sperling; previously an Anglican

RC Church

clergyman, and the father of A.M. Sperling, the priest at Leek from 1884 to 1923. Two bells, cast by Taylor and Co. of Loughborough, are given by the priest and his father. The church also possesses two pieces of Leek embroidery, an altar frontal and a cope. The church of 1864 becomes part of the school and is later used as the parish hall.

St Luke's Church is finished.

James Rider, printer and bookseller, is in Spout Street, and later at 6 Derby Street.

The tercentenary of Shakespeare's birth is celebrated by readings from his works in the Wesleyan Methodist school in West Street.

Benjamin Barlow, the organist at St Edward's Church, is involved in the formation of Leek and District Association for Promoting Church Music, which seeks to encourage congregational singing in Anglican churches.

Friendly societies renew their participation in Club Day.

The North Staffordshire Soda Water Works in Derby Street are run by Mrs Caroline Byrne.

Middleton's Marionette Theatre, a small tent theatre, opens in the cattle market.

1865 – End of the American Civil War

The Ragged School opens in a cottage in Belle Vue Road. (Originating in an idea of a Portsmouth shoemaker who taught deprived children without charge, The Ragged School Union was formed in 1844 under the patronage off Lord Shaftesbury.) The demand for places is great, and six weeks later the school moves to two adjoining houses in Mill Street.

Box making is still being done by Jabez Pickford but the business fails.

The Leek and Moorlands Co-operative Society changes its name to the Leek and Moorlands Industrial Provident Society Ltd.

Local craftsmen are making handlooms for domestic workers. Henry Hubbard is in business as a loom and silk machine maker in Union Street. Otherwise there is no evidence that textile machinery is made in Leek. Much of the machinery introduced into the mills in the late 19th and early 20th centuries came from abroad and was installed by foreign workers.

Robert Nall sells his printing business to William Clemesha, who had the first flatbed machine in Leek.

It is estimated that the various friendly societies and clubs had nearly 1,700 members, almost one fifth of the town's population.

The infants' school in Ball Haye Street is improved when six new classrooms are built and a schoolroom is heightened.

The Leek and Moorlands Subscription Library is taken over by another Leek bookseller, James Rider, who runs it from his shop in Derby Street.

Lawrence, the master of the Leek Grammar School, has twenty-four boys, four boarders, plus six or seven others who come from outside Leek. He teaches six poor boys free in return for an income (£9 13s. 10d.) from the Roades bequest, but the arrangement ends when Lawrence leaves. He is a good teacher, but cannot afford an assistant. He deals with boys of all ages, abilities and requirements. The schoolhouse is in poor repair and no longer suitable. There is little demand in Leek for a traditional grammarschool education. Those parents who want one send their sons elsewhere. Nevertheless, the Inspector for the Royal Commission on Grammar Schools recommends that the school should continue as a feeder for the high school in some other town.

The brewery attached to the Blue Ball, Mill Street is described as newly erected when advertised for lease. A month later the contents are put up for sale and are described as being the late property of a brewer named Marriott.

John Kipling marries Alice MacDonald (not in Leek) and together they leave for Bombay, where he takes up a position as the Head of the School of Art. Joseph Rudyard Kipling is born in Bombay.

Lord Macclesfield transfers the advowson to the bishop.

More cricket clubs are formed: the Recreation Club, the Congregational Church and the Gladstone Club. They all play at Beggars Lane. Leek CC is playing at Slater's Field (now Langford Street).

1866 – Leek Amateur Musical Society is founded. Mrs Cruso is an honorary member. The first concert is on 8 May in the Temperance Hall.

Reading is still taught at the Wesleyan Sunday school in Mill Street.

New Street is renamed Horton Street.

The premises of Alfred Overfield, cabinetmaker, burn down.

Spout Street is renamed as St Edward Street; Custard Street is renamed as Stanley Street.

John Davenport's grandson, George Davenport, sells Big Birchall to Howard Haywood.

After earlier unsuccessful attempts, trade unionism becomes established in the Leek silk industry. The Amalgamated Society of Silk Twisters is formed with William Stubbs as the secretary. Other societies follow.

The Bridge End brewery closes. Its stock, including beer and movables, is put up for sale.

No horse racing takes place in Leek this year.

J. and J. Brough, Nicholson and Co. have a warehouse built on the east side of Cross Street with a shade behind it, both to the design of William Sugden.

The Ragged School is held on Sundays and for two hours every weekday evening. There are 120 on the books. On Sundays, reading is taught by unpaid teachers. The average attendance is eighty. At night, there is a schoolmaster and mistress, each paid £6 a year. They teach writing and arithmetic, and the mistress also teaches the girls to sew.

Leek and Moorlands Cricket Club moves to the ground at Highfield Hall, given free by the owner, Arthur Nicholson.

1867 – The Leek Improvement Commissioners set about ensuring that all working children receive some schooling.

The firm of Wardle and Davenport is formed, in a partnership between Henry Wardle, the keeper of Britannia tavern in West Street, also described as a photographer, and George Davenport, a silk throwster. Wardle provides the capital, and Davenport runs the business. The premises are at first in West Street.

The July fair is by this time purely nominal.

There is a branch of the Post Office Savings Bank in Leek.

Robert Farrow (1822–1906), who settled in Leek in 1847, works as a tallow chandler, and becomes active in campaigns for sanitary reform.

John Cruso, the solicitor, dies, leaving a widow aged 55.

The Workshops Regulation Act becomes law.

The Leek Harmonic Brass Band is formed and holds Friday evening concerts in Market Place during the summer.

James Bostock manages Wombwell's Travelling Menagerie, James is eventually succeeded as manager by his son Edward, "*the British Barnum*".

The number of children attending school halftime has greatly increased. Leek teachers complain about halftime attendance and about the pressure put on the children by parents and employers to leave school for work in the mills.

The Plymouth Brethren register the Quaker Meeting House at Overton Bank for worship as "*persons who object to be designated by any distinctive sectarian appellation*".

The *Staffordshire Advertiser* states that the Highfield Hall Committee have worked with great zeal, being determined to ascertain if a "Belle Vue" would pay in Leek. ("Belle Vue" was a combined zoological park and pleasure ground which combined animals in cages with a funfair. It was on the outskirts of Manchester and easily accessible from Leek on the railway.)

Grosvenor Street is completed.

The Mechanics' Institute is free of debt.

The November fair includes a hiring fair.

The railway line is open from StokeuponTrent to the Churnet Valley railway at Leekbrook.

Workhouse Street is renamed Brook Street.

A Quaker evangelist is appointed, but he has little success.

Under the terms of the Factories Act, the inspection and enforcement duties are exercised by the local authority. The Leek Improvement Commissioners vest these powers in Robert Farrow, who is appointed as sanitary inspector. He continues to hold post under the Urban District Council, and also serves as supervisor of markets, the school attendance officer, and the secretary to the fire brigade.

Races are being held at Highfield Park.

The trustees of Ann Jolliffe's charity (see 1732) use the money to buy thirty-four-acre Pewit Hall farm, in Onecote.

Elizabeth Condlyffe buys land at Cornhill Cross as the site for six almshouses.

The town authorities take a sevenyear lease on the grounds at Highfield Hall, which is opened as a park for the town's working population. There is an entry charge of one penny The Committee provides facilities for bowling and croquet and encourages athletics by staging sports days on the first Sunday of each month. The first such day, in June, attracts 1,600 spectators. The park is also used for horse racing.

A new pulpit replaces the old pulpit when the chancel is rebuilt at St Edward's Church.

Milk Street, Prince Street and Pump Street are officially named.

The Privy Council licenses a fortnightly cattle market at Leek.

Children from the Congregational Church join in the Club Day walking.

There are five wood turners in Leek engaged in making bobbins.

At St Edward's Church a font is given in memory of John Cruso. The old 18th century font is transferred to Kirknewton church in Northumberland.

An additional race meeting is held at Highfield Park on Monday and Tuesday following the town's Club Day on the first Friday in August.

William Clemesha, printer, stationer and bookbinder at 11 Stanley Street, buys the business from George Nall and Son.

The first Annual Party of the Leek Co-operative movement is held at the Temperence Hall. Three hundred attend and the dividend is declared at 1s. 3d. in the pound.

George Davenport sells Westwood Hall, with much of the estate, to John Robinson.

There are 251 workshops in the town, devoted mainly to the production of sewing silk and employing 1,440 people.

George Ashton, clockmaker, moves to Compton.

In September, the British School for Boys opens in two rooms in a rented building in Union Street. By December the master has thirty-six pupils, who pay from tuppence to sixpence a week.

The Government's Science and Art Department support the School of Art set up that year by the Leek Mechanics' Institute. The tutor, hired from the Art School at StokeuponTrent, holds classes at the Institute and at the Union Street British School.

The Mechanics' Institute has fewer workingclass members than there had been. Efforts are made to enrol more. The full annual subscription, still described by managers as "*trifling*", had been increased to 12 shillings, and probably few of the new members were working men.

Ralph Mountfort is a grocer and twine manufacturer.

For some years, Jukes Worthington has been in partnership with Thomas Halcomb, his brotherinlaw. Thomas withdraws and Andrew's son Ernest becomes partner.

Leek Races become the North Staffordshire Races, with the autumn meeting at Leek.

Alfred Overfield, cabinetmaker, has his premises rebuilt.

Highfield Hall is leased for seven years by a party of gentlemen for use as a recreation ground. Admission will be one penny. A grandstand is erected, and a new course for Leek Races created, plus other sporting activities.

Challinor and Co. practise under that name.

The Union Workhouse School employs a master and mistress who attempt vocational training.

Norman Shaw comes to the area to design the rebuilding of Meerbrook Church.

A soup kitchen is built in Stockwell Street by the Improvement Commissioners. They let it to the Relief Committee, which has been dispensing soup since the beginning of the year. It lasts for four years.

The International Crispin Patent Boot and Shoe Co. Ltd wholesale business is established in London Street and is among the six most important boot and shoe manufacturers in Staffordshire.

A "*perpetual curacy*" styled vicarage is opened.

St Luke's School and Fountain Street are overcrowded, and threatened with loss of their government grant.

Part of the workhouse in Broad Street is being used as a dye-works.

F.A. Argles of Haregate and his wife help to maintain the day school run by an uncertificated teacher in a rented room at Ball Haye Green.

1869 – Mrs Cruso is appointed as the Treasurer of Leek Amateur Musical Society.

The Bridge End Brewery, on the Leekfrith side of the River Churnet, is being worked by William Brown Lea.

Following the retirement of Joshua and John Brough, a new partnership is formed between Joshua Nicholson, B.B. Nixon, W.S. Brough (Joshua Brough's son), Arthur Nicholson (Joshua Nicholsons younger son), Edwin Brough (John Brough's son) and John Hall (apprenticed to the firm in 1854).

The British School for Boys, Union Street, receives a government grant. Successive masters will also run a night school.

Mill Street Chapel and Ragged School opens.

The Leek Wesleyan Methodist quarterly meeting agrees to take charge of the Ragged School, following a request from the school's Committee of Management.

Jean Baptiste François Mien dies in Leek aged 84 (see 1804).

The Commissioners appoint the Fire Brigade Committee and set up a volunteer brigade in addition to the paid brigade. An engine is bought for the volunteer brigade, which is housed in Stockwell Street.

1870 – Highfield Hall is bought by Edwin Cliffe Glover, one of a Stoke family, from Sarah Fowler and her sons. Glover is the Vice President of Leek Cricket Club and allows the Club free use of the grounds.

William Spooner Brough is appointed the captain of the Volunteer Fire Brigade.

The leading architects in town are Larner Sugden and his father William.

Messrs Brough, Nicholson and Hall acquire Hope Mill in Fountain Street.

Travelling theatrical companies play in the cattle market at the east end of Derby Street.

A weekly *Leek Times* is founded by M.H. Miller. It is a paper that is politically neutral, although Miller himself is a Liberal.

A day school is established by the Wesleyan Methodists at Ball Haye Green.

Leek Cottage Hospital, known as the Alsop Memorial Hospital, at the east end of Stockwell Street opens. It is built by Adelina Alsop in memory of her husband James (d. 1868) on the land given by his nephews John and Robert Alsop JP. Designed by William Sugden, it consists of a male ward of four beds, a female ward of three beds and two cots, plus two private wards each with one bed.

The lease on Highfield Hall as a park is surrendered, for financial reasons. The public use of the park is discontinued after that year's autumn horse races on 8 and 9 August. Thereafter horse races at Highfield Hall are also discontinued.

In November, the loss of Highfield Park causes the Improvement Commissioners to take the lease of the land on the south side of Britannia Street for a recreation ground.

The Leek Amateur Dramatic Society is formed, but does not last.

Lawrence, the master of Leek Grammar School, is succeeded by Joseph Sykes, the master of the private Leek Commercial School. Shortly afterwards the income from the Roades charity is assigned to one of the town's National schools. Joseph Sykes and later John Sykes run the school for the next thirty years.

Attendance is poor at the Art Classes at the School of Art set up by the Leek Mechanics' Institute, and the classes are abandoned.

Animals, being offered for sale, are clogging the streets of the town.

1871 – William Clemesha is still postmaster.

The Plymouth Brethren cease to meet at the Quaker Meeting House at Overton Bank.

The Leek United Permanent Benefit Building Society moves to St Edward Street.

The west end of Southbank Street exists.

Six Italian bagpipe players are lodging in Leek, presumably itinerant entertainers.

The Leek Harmonic Brass Band plays in the Market Place on Monday evenings.

Mountfords are still working the Ball Haye Green ropewalk.

The Temperance Hall is enlarged by the addition of an orchestra pit and changing rooms.

The average attendance at the British School for Boys, Union Street, day school is over sixty. A pupil teacher is appointed.

A chapel opens in Mill Street as part of the building which also houses the Ragged School.

William Phillips, silk manufacturer, with a mill at Barngates, dies. His house, The Field, passes to Thomas Whittles.

Out of 2,072 children, aged five to thirteen, living in the area covered by the Leek Improvement Act of 1855, 1,275 are at school full time, 401 work in factories or workshops and attend school halftime, 102 work full time in trades where there still no legal obligation to ensure that child workers received some schooling, and there are fifty "*street arabs*". Of those aged 11 to 13 there 244 legally employed full time in factories or in silk winding or throwing.

The decision is taken to demolish the old Town Hall (at the bottom of Market Place) at the instigation of Joshua Brough.

F.A. Argles of Haregate and his wife build and settle in trust (that is, they leave enough money in trust to pay for its upkeep) the mixed and infants' day school in Pump Street. The new building is soon used as a mission church also. The site includes two cottages in Prince Street, which are assigned as residences for the teacher and the caretaker. The school has a certificated mistress. It soon has an average attendance of 51, and later in the year began to receive a government grant.

A schoolhouse, with rooms for boys, girls, and infants, is built behind the Roman Catholic church in King Street. The Methodist School moves into the newly built Wesleyan Methodist school and chapel in Mill Street.

Messrs Brough, Nicholson and Hall employ 470 persons.

The day school of the Wesleyan Methodists, at Ball Haye Green, has thirty pupils. A certificated mistress is appointed and the managers apply for a government grant.

Volunteers take charge of the fire escape (presumably a ladder of some sort!) belonging to the Commissioners.

1872 – Mathew Henry Miller is the editor and proprietor of the *Leek Times* in Stanley Street.

St Luke's Church possesses several pieces of Leek embroidery, some designed by J.D. Sedding of Bristol.

A meeting hall and classrooms, also designed by Sugden, are built in Russell Street.

The Company of Rifle Volunteers have a drill room, known as the Armoury, in Ford Street.

The Duchess of Teck and the Duke of Cambridge stay at Alton Towers and come to Leek by a special train. They are taken to the Roches, where a seat has been carved out of stone for the Princess to sit on. It is called "The Queen's Chair".

The partnership of the Commercial Bank is dissolved. R.R. Ellis is left to close the bank at heavy loss to himself.

A mixed day school with a government grant opens on the upper floor of the infants' school in Ball Haye Street.

A furnace is operated by Woodhead and Carter, and is known as the Hope Foundry. It is on the opposite side of Newcastle Road from the railway station.

William Michael Hilliard is still in business in Stockwell Street as auctioneer and appraiser.

Samuel Tatton is appointed postmaster with his premises in Stanley Street.

Wardle and Davenport have moved to part of the Big Mill in Mill Street, sharing it with William Broster and Co. and Frederick Hammersley and Co.

Omnibuses run from The Swan and The George to the railway station.

Wood Street exists.

There are two boxmakers in Leek.

There are two bobbin turners, George Plant in Mill Street and William Wain in Buxton Road.

Thomas Wardle buys, from Samuel Tatton, Hencroft dye-works in Abbey Green Road and the Mill Street dye-works, which are renamed the Churnet Works.

The Relief Committee is still dispensing soup from the soup kitchen in Stockwell Street.

The old Town Hall, at the bottom of the Market Square, is demolished and the stone sold to Mr Fowler and used for Portland House. Demolition cost £85.

With demolition of the old Town Hall, the Improvement Commissioners reerect the fountain in Canal (later Broad) Street.

Richard Cooper, in general practice in Leek, dies.

There is concern at the volunteers' lack of shooting skill, which leads to the formation of the Leek Volunteer Shooting Club, with butts on the land to the south of Wall Grange Farm.

Mark Abbott, the ropemaker, still lives in Buxton Road.

All Saints' Church of England School is extended. It is a school initially run as an infants' school and receives a government grant as such, but is also taking older children. In the winter, the mistress runs the night school and the day school in Pump Street.

Night classes stop at the British School for Boys, Union Street, when it is abandoned for lack of support.

The new boys' school at St Luke's School, designed by William Sugden, is completed, with entrances in Queen Street and Earl Street. It is for girls and infants. One hundred and fifty remain in the Fountain Street building.

A newsroom for working men opens at Ball Haye Green.

The Conservative Association is formed.

The Commissioners take the lease of springs at Upper Hulme.

A Rose Society is established.

1873 – St Luke's Church chancel is extended by 10 feet. Its floor is laid with Minton tiles, and a reredos of Caen stone is erected. The work is designed by J.D. Sedding of Bristol, and most of the cost is met by C.H. Joberns, formerly an assistant curate.

The club that will later become Leek Town Football Club is formed.

Jukes Worthington dies.

A newsroom for working men is opened at No. 13 Market Place.

Norman Shaw designs Spout Hall in St Edward Street, the house of John Sleigh, author of *A History of the Ancient Parish of Leek*, published in 1862.

A Meeting is held at the Swan Hotel to establish a Rugby Football Club, in connection with Leek Cricket Club.

A separate infants' school is formed at St Lukes School.

Hargreaves School is built, but not opened. It is named in honour of George Hargreaves, for many years a trustee of the Congregational Chapel.

Premises of Congregationalists of Union Street become a girls' and infants' school and began to receive a government grant.

Membership of the Mechanics' Institute peaks at 305. The Institute's main attractions are its library and reading room.

The two fire brigades merge as a single volunteer brigade.

Benjamin Barlow, the organist and choirmaster at St Edward's, dies. He was well known in Leek and throughout Staffordshire as a musician, choirmaster and music teacher.

The Ragged School becomes a public elementary day school known as the Mill Street Wesleyan School.

A band called "Talbot" play on Thursday evenings in the cattle market at the east end of Derby Street.

The Leek Harmonic Brass Band changes its name to the Leek Promenade Band.

Ball Haye Green Working Men's Institute is established. It is not known where the institute first met.

In the town there are 325 water closets as against 650 privies.

Under Ann Jolliffe's charity (see 1732), land at Compton is exchanged for 36 acres at the Rock Tenement farm at Wetley Rocks.

1874 – The Leek and Moorlands Cricket Club decide to return to Beggars Lane. This leads to a dispute, and a new club called Leek Highfield is formed by those who prefer not to move back.

The Commissioners open the Smithfield in Haywood Street, banning all livestock sales in the streets. The site at the end of Derby Street continues to be used as an overflow Smithfield and also as a fairground and venue for the travelling theatrical companies until the Monument is built there.

Workhouse Street has been extended to London Road as Haywood Street.

The last French POW to stay in Leek dies.

The death rate in Leek is 15.5 per 1,000 per annum.

The Bridge End brewery, building and equipment are not in use when they are offered for sale.

Mrs Alsop, who managed and maintained the hospital herself, hands it over to a committee for three years. During that time she continues to maintain the building and contributes towards the running of the hospital, which is also supported by subscriptions and donations.

The nave and aisles of St Edward's Church are re-seated with open benches instead of box pews to a plan prepared by Mr Street, the architect.

Land in Leonard Street adjoining the cattle market is used as the town yard for storing materials.

A carillon (a set of bells for the playing of tunes and/or the mechanism for playing them) is made at St Edward's Church by Gillett and Bland of Croydon and installed by subscription. It consists of fourteen tunes, one of which is played four times in the course of each day.

On 17 January, Leek Football Club hold their first practice match at the White Lion ground at Bridge End.

The Improvement Commissioners install a clock by Gillett and Bland at St Edward's Church.

The Improvement Commissioners open an isolation hospital in temporary premises on the west side of Ashbourne Road.

The Mechanics' Institute starts new classes in science and art, again in connection with the Science and Art Department. Art classes, taught by the headmaster of Hanley School of Art, are at first well attended.

Dampier Street and Hugo Street are laid out.

Joseph Needham is recorded as a printer. His premises are on the corner of Derby Street and Market Place.

The public baths are taken over by the Improvement Commissioners under the Public Health Act of 1872.

1875 – Messrs Brough, Nicholson and Hall double the size of Hope Mill.

The Nicholson Institute is conceived as a monument to free-trade campaigner Richard Cobden.

Leek Co-op shops open during the daytime.

Robert Farrow, the Sanitary Inspector to the Improvement Commissioners, states that very little handloom weaving survives.

The industrial and educational legislation has made it difficult to secure helpers, boys being at their most useful between the ages of nine and fourteen and turning to other work after fifteen or sixteen.

The first part of Leonard Street, running south from Haywood Street, is completed.

The area to the south of the town centre is developed.

The New Connexion Methodists chapel at the corner of Ball Haye Street and Queen Street is known as the Bethesda Chapel.

Compton school church has its own wardens.

At a conference William Challinor is able to claim that Leek, from having been one of the worst towns in sanitary matters twenty years before, had become one of the best and that its death rate of about 30 in 1,000 in 1860 had fallen to 15½.

The mission church of St John the Evangelist in Mill Street, opened as a branch of St. Edward's schools, becomes a school church. It is built at the expense of John Robinson of Westwood Hall.

Sir Thomas Wardle brings William Morris to Leek to experiment on dyes.

Newsrooms for working men are opened in the former soup kitchen in Stockwell Street.

Leek continues to expand steadily. The silk industry is concentrated in factories, and several firms are established. Leek also has increased importance as a market town.

The town is involved in the shortlived Cambridge University extension scheme in North Staffordshire. Courses of lectures on chemistry and on history are given at Leek. At the end of the session thirteen people are awarded certificates by examination.

Congregationalists open a mixed and infants' school with twenty-four pupils in a building erected in Alsop Street.

Samuel Tatton leaves Hencroft (as Wardle's tenant) and moves to Britannia Street.

Death of William Travis, the clockmaker of the Market Place.

Mr Davenport senior retires from Wardle and Davenport and is succeeded by Henry Davenport.

The last quarter of the century sees an increasing concentration of the silk industry in factories.

Ernest Worthington and his brother Philip are in partnership with Henry Russell, a London silk agent.

William Morris becomes a frequent visitor to the Hencroft works. Wardle's brotherinlaw, George Wardle, is the manager of Morris's works in London. With Morris, Thomas Wardle revives indigo dyeing and restores vegetable dyes to an important place in the industry. Their business association lasts until the early 1880s. Thomas Wardle also promotes the use of Indian wild silks, especially that of the tusser worm, dyed at the Churnet works under the supervision of his son Arthur; and woven silk, printed at the Hencroft works under another son, Bernard.

1876 – The executors of Martha Babington give £50, the interest to be spent on paying each almswoman 5 shillings a year on 1 January.

The fountain given by William Challinor and designed by Joseph Durham is erected on the site of the town hall.

There are four box makers in Leek.

The Benevolent Burial Society is the largest friendly society, with 7,545 members. It becomes a general insurance society.

Nicholson Institute

Challinor Fountain

The Improvement Commissioners are represented on the schoolattendance committee of the Leek PoorLaw Union.

The Leek and Moorlands Bicycle Club is formed.

About 650 factory hands and outworkers are engaged in the town's shoe trade.

A school of cookery is formed in connection with the National School for Cookery at South Kensington. It originally meets in the Rifle Volunteers' Hall in Ford Street.

The mission opens in Alsop Street School.

Ashbourne Road is disturnpiked.

St. John's C.E. School, Mill Street is made independent of St. Edward's schools and begins to receive a government grant. The average attendance is 66.

Leek Volunteers Corps form a Rugby Football Club.

On 9 December, the Challinor Fountain is presented to the town.

The International Crispin Patent Boot and Shoe Co. Ltd closes.

On 1 June, a skating rink opens at Rudyard.

1877 – On 25 June, Captain Webb visits Rudyard to take part in a Grand Aquatic Entertainment. There is a crowd of over 20,000. The crowd is disappointed that he only swims about!

The building on the Ashbourne Road side of Smithfield is bought and converted into the Coffee Tavern with a room for transacting business.

Mrs Alsop hands the Cottage Hospital over to the trustees.

Larner Sugden designs his own house at no. 29 Queen Street.

At the Armoury in Ford Street, a reading room and gymnasium are added.

Maria Jane Van Tuyl, by will, leaves £1,000 for the almswomen.

During the winter, a mistress runs the night school and the day school in Pump Street.

The Roman Catholic school receives a government grant. The average attendance is 106 and the staff consists of two nuns and three assistants.

The National School for Cookery begins to sponsor courses of lectures and cookery demonstrations at the Temperance Hall in Union Street.

The day school in Pump Street is extended, at Mr Argles's expense.

Leek Football Club adopts Association Rules. The first match, on 20 January, is against Uttoxeter. They lose 0-1.

F.W. Jennings sells his Stockwell Street Bank to Warringtonbased Parr's Banking Co. Ltd.

1878 – The Sandon to Bullock Smithy road is disturnpiked. The Sheephouse tollhouse is put up for sale.

Leek Total Abstinence Society supports the opening of the Coffee House in the Haywood Street cattle market.

The recreation ground is bought for building purposes and ultimately becomes Chorley Street and Gladstone Street.

G.H. Plant and Sons, box makers, are established in Mill Street.

Three new streets are laid out: Cromwell Terrace, Livingstone Street and Talbot Street.

There is a new fourbedroomed house built by the entrance to Horton Street Mill.

There are brickworks east of Compton, along with sand and gravel working.

Three streets, named after Leonard Haywood Shoobridge, who owns the land, are built.

Additions are made to Ballington House.

Another evangelist is engaged to take services in the mission in Alsop Street School.

R. Sleigh of Leek plays for Stoke Football Club in the 1877/78 season.

Fred Adams buys a small dairy farm from the Earl of Macclesfield.

Rules for a nonpolitical and nonsectarian organisation called "The Union Club" are drawn up on temperance principles. The club's meeting place is Union Buildings, Market Street.

Union Buildings in Market Street are built "*to supply rational recreation without the temptation of drink*". Designed by Alfred Waterhouse and others, they are principally a concert hall, but also contain games rooms and a restaurant. The venture was not a success.

At the Leek Grammar School, a department for girls and small boys is opened under Miss M.L. Sykes.

The Leek and District Civic Society is formed to monitor the architectural heritage and the development of the town and an area covering former townships in Leek ancient parish, together with Bagnall, Cheddleton, Consall, Horton and Ipstones.

The National School for Cookery cooperates in a scheme which provides workers with hot midday meals, eaten at its new premises in Stockwell Street or taken away.

Elizabeth Condlyffe dies.

Opening of the Coffee Tavern.

The sixty-four-acre Dee Bank farm in Mount Road is acquired by the Town Lands Trustees from John Robinson of Westwood Hall in exchange for nineteen acres at Westwood.

The lease on land off Britannia Street for use as a park is surrendered, and the land is bought for housing. Gladstone Street and Chorley Street are laid out.

Both the mixed and infants' schools in Ball Haye Street are threatened with the loss of their government grants unless the building is improved. Considerable alterations are made

1879 – Battles of Isandlwana and Rorke's Drift

Leek Co-op has large premises in Ashbourne Road.

The Leek and Moorland Bicycle Club is formed.

The Westwood Recreation Ground opens.

At the British School for Boys, Union Street, attendance sometimes exceeds 150, and an assistant master is engaged.

The Leek and Moorlands Permanent Benefit Building Society is incorporated as the Leek and Moorlands Building Society.

Leek Town FC play Ashbourne away "*under floodlights*".

Art Classes at the School of Art, set up by the Leek Mechanics' Institute, move from the institute to a hired room in Stockwell Street, which is large but badly lit and poorly ventilated. The Science and Art Department threaten to withdraw its grant unless better premises are found.

The Leek branch of the Charity Organization Society is formed with an office in Silk Street.

The Magistrates' Court leaves the West Street Wesleyan School and moves to Union Buildings in Market Street. Later they move to the Town Hall.

The Commissioners lay out the five-acre recreation ground between Westwood Road and Spring Gardens.

Grove Street is extended further and Westwood Grove is laid out with building plots.

Mr Wardle retires from Wardle and Davenport.

On 24 March, the Leek Amateur Musical Society performs *Elijah*.

Newcastle road is disturnpiked.

1880 – Buttons covered in a mixture of silk and mohair are still being produced by about 300 people in Leek and neighbouring villages, notably at Flash and Biddulph Moor, and continue to be the staple of Leek's textile industry.

J.W. Jennings, retired banker, dies.

1879 - Co-Op
Ashbourne Road

The Brunswick School in Regent Street is built.

Leek Co-op starts a penny bank.

George Massey is making ginger beer in Shoobridge Street.

The town is described as both the Metropolis and the Queen of the Moorlands.

Ball Haye Green Football Club is formed.

Chorley Street and Gladstone Street are built on the former recreation ground bought for the purpose.

William Wain is still in business turning bobbins.

William Spooner Brough, son of Joshua Brough, builds a house on the opposite side of Buxton Road to Abbotts Road to his father's house and calls it Littlehales. Larner Sugden combines brick with timber framing.

Dye-works are added on the opposite side of Horton Street Mill using water from Ball Haye brook.

Larner Sugden designs 33 and 35 Bath Street.

An assistant master starts the night school again at the British School for Boys, Union Street. The day school is overcrowded. Another room is added to the school.

Hargreaves School has an average attendance of 100.

As part of a national movement to improve methods of embroidery, Elizabeth Wardle, wife of Leek silk dyer Thomas Wardle, establishes a Leek Embroidery Society (also known later as Leek School of Embroidery). Using naturally dyed silks or other materials from the Wardle factory, the society produced both designs and finished articles.

Leek and Moorlands Subscription Library has closed.

The fourbedroomed house by the entrance to the Horton Street Mill becomes the home of William Stannard after he acquires the mill.

The railway station is rebuilt.

Samuel Tatton, the postmaster, has moved to St Edward Street.

The Leek and Moorlands Co-operative Society opens a branch shop and bakery in Ashbourne Road. Other branches follow.

The Improvement Commissioners build a permanent hospital on the west side of Ashbourne Road. The four wards can accommodate twenty patients.

William Clemesha has moved to St Edward Street.

The Leek Quakers meeting is revived.

The traditional sport of heaving (it is not certain what this involved but it could be the throwing of a heavy sheaf of corn or hay over a high pole) in Easter week has ceased, but the custom of dragging a plough on Plough Monday (the Monday after Twelfth Night) is still being observed.

The first spun silk comes from W.S. Watson and Co.

On 15 May, Leek Cricket Club play Burton upon Trent and score 368 runs, a club record.

The chapels at Meerbrook, Onecote and Rushton Spencer have parishes assigned to them.

1881 – Messrs Brough, Nicholson and Hall are employing 630 people.

Vicars Close, consisting of 2½ acres on the Newcastle road, is sold.

The West Street day school is extended.

The average attendance at the Art Classes at the School of Art, set up by the Leek Mechanics' Institute has fallen to thirty.

Joshua Nicholson is persuaded to add accommodation for an art school to his projected institute at Leek. An independent committee is formed to manage classes and to superintend their eventual move into the new institute.

The Manchester and Liverpool District Bank moves temporarily into Gaunt House on the other side of Derby Street while its premises are rebuilt.

St. John's C.E. School, Mill Street, is enlarged. The Congregationalists take over the school's management, running it in conjunction with their school in Alsop Street and the Congregationalist school in Union Street.

George Hill starts a stationery and printing business in Stanley Street.

Wardle's son Arthur joins the firm.

Larner Sugden is taken into the partnership with his father, William Sugden. He widens the practice and is responsible for the Queen Anne style of many of its later buildings, which also display considerable eclecticism. He is living at Woodcroft House.

Southbank Street is extended to Compton.

W.S. Brough retires.

The Commissioners take over rooms in the Union Buildings in Market Street.

The Overton Bank Leek Co-op shop becomes the boot and shoe department.

John Robinson of Westwood Hall pays for extensions to the mission church of St John the Evangelist in Mill Street.

The West Street School is enlarged. The architect is Larner Sugden.

The Wesleyans have also opened a room in Haywood Street for the Hallelujah Band Mission.

Bank, Derby Street

Architect Larner Sugden begins to publish essays and lectures by various authors under the general title of "Leek Bijou Freethought Reprints".

Canal Street is renamed Broad Street.

1882 – John Robinson is appointed as the Sheriff of the County. He is the last to be accompanied by the "Javelin Men". The javelins were later kept at Westwood Hall.

Four new firms appear: Henry Brassington of Grosvenor Street, who is also a paper merchant and a commission agent; Isaac Creighton of Cromwell Terrace and Shoobridge Street; John and Jabez Mathews of Buxton Road, who are also joiners and builders; and Murfin and Sons of London Mills, London Street.

Missions open at Ball Haye Green.

The Russell Street premises of the Commissioners are reopened as the Liberal Club.

Congregationalists transfer the boys from the Hargreaves mixed school in Alsop Street to the British School, Union Street.

The North Staffordshire Soda Water Works in Derby Street, run by Mrs Caroline Byrne, moves to Cross Street.

The Leek Co-op open their first branch shop at Ball Haye Green.

The Leek Savings Bank, at the corner of Russell Street and Derby Street, closes.

Mountfords are still working the Ball Haye Green ropewalk.

The Leek Amateur Musical Society perform their 50th concert.

Production of spun silk (thread made from silk waste) is introduced in Leek by William Watson and Co. Several local manufacturers, including Thomas Wardle, promptly combine to form the Leek Spun Silk Spinning and Manufacturing Co.

St Luke's Church parish magazine is first published.

The Salvation Navy registers a "harbour" in London Street. The registration is cancelled two months later.

The Leek and Moorlands Bicycle Club changes its name to the Leek Cyclists' Club.

Some friendly societies again parade.

Eight almshouses are built in what later becomes Condlyffe Road. They consist of two ranges joined by an arch, in an Arts and Crafts style designed by an architect named Lowe. Residence is restricted to men and women aged fifty years or over who are members of the Church of England.

Wombwell's Travelling Menagerie visits Leek.

The town's twelve public day schools have an average attendance of 2,043: 960 attended Anglican schools, 615 Wesleyan, 363 Congregationalist, and 105 Roman Catholic.

The Liberal Club at 8 Russell Street moves next door into the building recently vacated by the town's Improvement Commissioners and remodelled for the club by W. Sugden and Son.

A Friday market is introduced.

Henry Davenport enters into partnership with his brother George, who is already the manager.

A separate infants' department is established at St. John's C.E. School, Mill Street.

The Court Leet is discontinued.

1883 – Thomas Shaw joins the firm of Challinor and Co.

The United Christian Army registers the Mission Hall in Strangmans Walk. The registration is cancelled later the same year.

All Saints' C.E. school is extended

Sleigh's *History of Leek* is published.

Eleven cast-iron mileposts are erected on the Leek to Buxton road.

Horse racing is revived with the Birchall Dale course being used.

At the request of employers, the town's Improvement Commissioners abolish Wakes Week as a holiday, substituting the first Friday in August (Club Day) and the three following working days.

The Plymouth Brethren are still active in the town.

Thomas Wardle and W.S. Brough open a shop in Bond Street in London but it is shortlived. They also have a shop in St Edward Street, next to Wardle's home.

The Leek Philothespian Club is founded to perform plays and give recitations. They perform in public twice yearly, usually in the Temperance Hall.

New premises for the Manchester and Liverpool District Bank, designed by W. Sugden and Son, are opened, made of brick with stone dressings. The interior of the portico has frieze of tiles by William de Morgan. A notable feature is the firstfloor oriel window surmounted by a pediment containing the bank's coat of arms, thought to have been copied from the building by Norman Shaw in Leadenhall Street, London; the parent company.

The fire brigade is reorganised as a paid brigade following the resignation of W.S. Brough, the captain of the volunteer brigade.

In February, Robert West, the watchmaker at 29 Market Place (now demolished). erects a clock at his premises at his own expense.

1884 – Oscar Wilde, lecturing in Leek, pays tribute to Wardle's dyeing and to Leek's special contribution to the decorative arts. The meeting is at the Temperence Hall and the audience is described as "*small*".

On 16 October, the Nicholson Institute is officially opened. The first book from the library is lent to Mrs Cruso. The Institute includes three large rooms for the Art School, for which the school's Managing Committee pays a nominal rent. The headmaster is appointed and the school established on a permanent basis. Almost half of the cost of the furniture and equipment is raised by a bazaar held in the Town Hall, the rest cming from donations, Science and Art Department grants and the profits from the lecture given by Oscar Wilde. Besides art classes some practical and technical instruction is offered. Its free library makes the Mechanics' Institute less popular. The Nicholson Institute combines a free library, a museum, three picture galleries and premises for Leek's School of Art. The library contains about 6,000 volumes chosen by J.O. Nicholson, eldest son of Joshua Nicholson, open to all adults living within six miles of Leek. It is designed by Larner Sugden, in the Queen Anne style.

The Leek United Permanent Benefit Building Society is incorporated.

The Commissioners buy the whole of Union Buildings in Market Street, which then becomes the Town Hall.

Leek has five silk-dyeing firms, and some 300 to 400 people are employed in silk dyeing.

Girls are transferred from the Hargreaves School to the Congregationalist School in Union Street, and the boys at the British School moved to Alsop Street. Thereafter the school, known at first as the British School and from beginning of the 20th century simply as the Alsop Street School, remains a boys' and infants' school.

The Primitive Methodist Chapel at the west end of Fountain Street is rebuilt.

Leek Bijou Freethought Reprints publish (inter alia) *Art and Socialism* by William Morris.

At St Luke's Church, the vicar's income has risen to £265.

The Leek Progressive Club is established, with architect Larner Sugden as its secretary. It meets in Silk Street but proves to be shortlived.

The Union Club closes when the premises are sold, if not earlier.

The Committee of the Nicholson Institute organises educational lectures on literary, artistic and scientific subjects.

Richard Massey has taken over the business of George Massey in Shoobridge Street, moving it to Leonard Street.

The founders of the Leek Embroidery Society did not conceive it as commercial business, but demand has been such that some of the profit is used to employ embroideresses. Items are sold in London through the shop in Bond Street and later through agencies.

William Beresford, vicar from 1882 to 1919, starts a Young Men's Society at St Luke's Church.

Thomas Wardle states that there are now few cottage handlooms to be found.

Magistrates are also using the courtroom at the offices of Challinor and Co., solicitors of Derby Street.

Samuel Tatton, the postmaster, has moved to the former Savings Bank premises in Derby Street.

A Conservative weekly, *The Leek Post*, is founded. At first it is published by the North Staffordshire Newspaper Co. Ltd and produced in Pickwood Road.

There is a protest that the river between Leek and Rocester is being contaminated by the effluent from the print and dye works and by Leek's sewage, with a consequent threat to fishing.

1885 – Woodcroft Hall is owned by Henry Davenport.

The Leek Parliamentary Division covering north-east Staffordshire is created as one of seven new divisions for the county. The first MP is a Liberal.

The Chancel of St Edward's Church is remodelled by George Edmund Street.

Death of Joshua Nicholson, silk manufacturer.

Leek Rural District is created with offices at the premises of Challinors and Shaw, solicitors, 10 Derby Street.

Haregate Hall is owned by Ernest Andrew Worthington JP, silk manufacturer.

Parr's Bank move to new premises in St Edward Street on the site of the former Plough Inn, now Bank House. It is designed by W. Owen of Warrington.

The Mill Street Wesleyan School becomes an infants' school.

Enoch Hill continues his printing business after joining the Leek United Permanent Benefit Building Society as a clerk at the age of twenty.

West Street mixed and infants' school has 458 children.

Death of Joshua Brough.

William Spooner Brough inherits Buxton Villa, and lives there until his death.

Important changes start to take place in the industry's products and technology.

Henry Russell dies. The Worthington brothers continue in partnership.

Hugh Sleigh and Joseph Challinor promote the building of All Saints' Church in Compton, designed by Norman Shaw and decorated by members of the Arts and Crafts movement.

A monthly magazine from the Mission Centre is introduced.

Compton School Church is replaced as a church by All Saints' Church on the site on the corner of Southbank Street and Compton, part of which was given by Joseph Challinor of Compton House, the Leek solicitor. The foundation stone is laid. Compton School Church has been enlarged twice to more than double its original size.

The rectangularshafted cross to the south of St Edward's Church is set up there after lying for several years in three pieces against the east wall of the churchyard. It has a fragment of runic inscription and may date from the early 9th century. The roundshafted cross southeast the of church is a particularly fine and well-preserved example of its type, dating perhaps from the later 10th century. Inside the church are the remains of a wheelhead of a cross and also stone from a rectangular shaft with a carving perhaps depicting Christ carrying the Cross.

1886 – Private foundation of Leek's first secondary school for girls.

The Chamber of Commerce, consisting mainly of silk manufacturers, is established, but does not flourish.

The Hope Foundry is still in Newcastle Road when taken over by William Woodhead.

The National School for Boys is designed by J.G. Smith and opens in Britannia Street. The boys at the St Edward's National schools, Clerk Bank, are transferred there. The Clerk Bank building is left to girls and infants. The average attendance there over the next few years is 170.

A plan for an extension to the Hope Foundry is prepared by W. Sugden and Son.

The Conservatives win the Parliamentary seat.

William Michael Hilliard gives up his business as bookseller, stationer and printer and moves to Stockwell Street as an auctioneer and appraiser.

Edwin Cliffe Glover of Highfield Hall dies. Arthur Nicholson buys the Hall.

1887 – Queen Victoria's Golden Jubilee

St Mary's Catholic Church is built. The architect is A. Vivars. The King Street premises become the parish hall. One third of St Mary's opens.

A school church dedicated to the Good Shepherd opens at Thorncliffe.

All Saints' C.E. school continues to be used for worship until the opening of All Saints' Church.

The Salvation Army barracks in Haywood Street are registered for worship.

Pickwood recreation ground plus five acres is presented to the town by William Challinor of Pickwood on the occasion of Queen Victoria's jubilee.

The Conservative Association moves to new premises on the site of the Church Inn in Church Street, designed in the Tudor style by J.G. Smith.

The decoration of All Saints' (architect Richard Norman Shaw) starts. The reredos, given by Hugh Sleigh, is a triptych showing the Crucifixion, the paintings are by R. Hamilton Jackson, the frames are designed by W.R. Lethaby, the glass is mainly by Morris and Co. from designs by Sir Edward BurneJones, two windows in the south aisle are respectively by Gerald Horsley and J.E. Platt, the wall paintings in the chancel are by Horsley and are given by Hugh Sleigh, those in the Lady Chapel are by Horsley and by Platt, and the font and pulpit are thought to have been designed by Lethaby. The church possesses many pieces of Leek embroidery, including a funeral pall designed by Horsley.

All Saints' Church is consecrated. It is built of Kniveden stone. Challinor contributes nearly one third of the cost, and grants are made by the Lichfield Diocesan Church Extension Society and Incorporated Church Building Society. All sittings are free. The dedication to All Saints was chosen because an earlier choice, St Mary, was already the dedication of the nearby Roman Catholic church.

All Saints' Church (Photo: Mark Titterton)

The Nicholson Institute is supported from the rates, the town's Improvement Commissioners having adopted the Public Libraries Act of 1855.

W.B. Wright, the priest in charge of All Saints' from 1882 and the vicar from 1889 to 1921, describes himself as practising "*a quiet Catholic (as opposed to Protestant and Roman) ritual*" and All Saints' has continued in the High Church tradition.

The vicar has a glebe of 35 acres, with an estimated rental of £51.

A Mission opens in Angle Street.

Lectures are given at the Nicholson Institute in connection with the Oxford University extension scheme which runs in North Staffordshire from 1887 to 1892.

Cheese fairs are held in February, August, and October

1888 – Jack the Ripper

The Leek and Moorlands troop, part of The Queen's Own Royal Yeomanry, is disbanded.

The pollution of the River Churnet with sewage from outfalls as well as with effluent from the dye-works is causing concern.

Congregationalist schools have an average attendance of 140.

The town's first secondary school for girls is a private school on Overton Bank run by Edith Milner.

Mrs Mary Burne is making soda water in Fountain Street.

The Saturday market lapses.

Henry Brassington moves into London Mills. He is now solely a bobbin turner, having given up his other interests.

The third partner for Wardle and Davenport is W. H. Rider. The three partners buy the whole of Big Mill from W.A.L. Hammersley, with another mill to the southeast in Belle Vue being erected by Hammersley's father, W.H. Hammersley, on land adjoining the two buildings. The whole site occupies nearly 3½ acres.

There is a printing firm of Clemesha and Clowes.

The venue of the Leek Amateur Musical Society concerts moves from the Temperance Hall to the Town Hall in Market Street.

Sunday evening lectures given by Jeremiah Barnes, the assistant curate of St Edward's, come to an end.

1889 – The Bird in Hand is built in Market Square.

The parish of All Saints' is formed out of St Luke's and St Edward's, to cover the southern part of town and Longsdon. The new parish takes over, from Endon church, the responsibility for the mission at Longsdon. The patronage of the vicarage is vested in Joseph Challinor for life, with the reversion to the bishop.

Portland Street is extended south to London Road.

The first knitting machine using the latch needle is introduced.

When Edith Milner decides to close the girls' private school on Overton Bank, a committee of Anglicans and Nonconformists is set up to continue it as a nonsectarian high school.

The average attendance at the day school in Pump Street has risen to 125.

Although it has continued its educational work, the Mechanics' Institute has gradually become little more than a middleclass social club with a circulating library.

The annual Venison Feast is still being held.

The Leek Improvement Commissioners set up a technical instruction committee, shortly after the passing of the Technical Instruction Act.

Mary Flint leaves £500 for the almswomen.

The race meeting, having failed to attract sufficient visitors, is discontinued.

The girls' grammar school is being run in conjunction with the grammar school.

1890 – The County Council threatens proceedings against the Improvement Commissioners.

The law firm becomes Messrs Challinors and Shaw.

The Commissioners buy nearly five acres to the west of the cemetery.

Mill Street Works passes from George to Thomas Plant, who runs it for a short time.

William Spooner Brough lays out the Waste, north of the junction of Buxton Road and Novi Lane, and gives it to the town for recreational purposes. He also lays out the garden next to Littlehales and opens it to the public. In addition he plants an avenue of trees along Buxton Road.

L. Whittles and Son open a steam mill in Strangman's Walk (later Strangman Street).

Attendance at the art classes at the School of Art at the Nicholson Institute has fallen to 138.

The Leek Orchestral Society is formed.

James Rogers in Spout Street and Simeon Rogers in Queen Street close their ropewalk.

A house in Compton Terrace, formerly occupied by Eliza Bradshaw, is presented as a vicarage house in memory of her.

Miller's *Old Leeke* is published.

Leek Co-op opens a bakehouse.

Artificial silk is introduced, with Wardle and Davenport among the pioneers.

There are a few silk brokers in business in the town. They were at their most numerous in 1880s and 1890s when there were five or six.

1891 – Mr Nixon retires from Messrs Brough, Nicholson and Hall, and the firm has Arthur Nicholson and John Hall as partners.

Picton Street exists.

The Sugden firm designs additions to Woodcroft Hall.

The population of Leek and Lowe has grown steadily to reach 12,760.

The Leek Federation of Local Trades Unions is formed.

All Saints' C.E. school is extended.

St. Luke's Church vestry is built.

Hartington Street is built.

The Leek Improvement Commissioners adopts the 1889 Technical Instruction Act and starts its own classes in the Nicholson Institute as the Leek Technical School, complementing those offered by the Committee of what has become the Leek School of Art and Science. The Science and Art Department refuses to sanction government grants to two separate committees running similar courses in the same building.

1892 – Leek Golf Club is created.

The precursor of Leek Town FC plays on a pitch in the grounds of Highfield Hall.

The Leek Federation of Local Trades Unions promotes a series of lectures, including one by George Bernard Shaw on socialism.

Thomas Monk, a book printer, has premises in Leek.

Leek Alexandra Football Club is formed.

Enoch Hill is a printer at 6 Cawdrey Buildings.

Number 8 Stockwell Street is the shop of John Fallon, a greengrocer and poulterer.

Joseph Howard is still at 24 Market Place (see 1829) (this is probably his son of the same name).

A house in Pickwood Road is being used as a Mission Centre.

The girls' nonsectarian high school is in Queen Street.

The School of Art and Science and the Technical School merge with the approval of the Science and Art Department, as the Leek School of Art Science and Technology. The average weekly attendance is 354.

1893 – The new police station designed by W. Sugden and Son opens in Leonard Street, with a superintendent's house attached.

The National Telephone Co. opens an exchange in Stockwell Street.

A plot of land is added to the site of the Cottage Hospital.

The panelling in the chancel of St Luke's Church is given by Susannah Argles and the choir stalls are given by the family of A.J. Worthington.

In Cross Street, Brough's mill has been extended north to the junction with Well Street to the design of Larner Sugden.

Thomas Rihes is a tailor and outfitter at Norfolk House, 12 Market Place.

George Davenport sells Barnfields Farm to Joseph Challinor

Death of William Sugden.

California Mill is so named.

The North Street area and corresponding part of Westwood Road is built.

The North Staffordshire Soda Water Works in Cross Street are taken over by Moses Heapy, a Fountain Street grocer.

The Leek Cricket Club professional, C. Rothera, aged 28, collapses and dies during a match.

Enoch Hill has moved the printing business into a shop in Cawdry Buildings, Fountain Street, where he also has a bookselling and stationery business. He employs his three brothers in the printing side of business. He later becomes prominent in the building society movement, After being a twister's helper and a farm labourer, he worked for two Leek printers and installed a press in his home.

The grammar school has about sixty-five pupils

1894 – The British Fern Society is established, promoted by John Robinson of Westwood Hall.

Mrs Cruso dies on 1 October.

George Davenport of Wardle and Davenport buys Foxlowe.

The arched entrance gateway, designed by W. Sugden and Son, is added to the Cottage Hospital, the gift of Mrs Alsop, with the gates given by John Robinson, the Chairman of the Committee. They are later removed to allow ambulances to drive up to the main door.

Isabella Carr, the daughter of Thomas Carr, the Leek silk manufacturer, has three almshouses built at the east end of Fountain Street in memory of her sisters Ellen and Rosanna Carr. Residence is restricted to men and women, whether married or single, who are members of the Church of England.

The children from the Roman Catholic Church participate in Club Day. Roman Catholic children could take part because the festival was not regarded as an act of worship, there being hymns but no prayers.

A firm called Clowes and Co. has a printing works in London Street.

Daintry Street is built.

Flat knitting machines are being used. Some existing firms add knitted goods to their products.

Barngate Street and Cruso Street have been built.

A small sample of artificial silk is received in Leek, and people are asked to report on its utility to be made into braid. It is reported that the sample is too small to form an opinion.

Leek Cricket Club joins the North Staffordshire League.

The Leek Amateur Musical Society holds a sale of work to raise funds.

Just over one acre of the cemetery is consecrated by the Bishop of Lichfield.

The Missions at Ball Haye Green are closed.

A Men's Club is started with a clubroom, opposite the vicarage.

There is a demand for beaded galloons (a narrow tape-like trimming or binding material).

The Volunteers use the upper storey of a converted building in Haywood Street cattle market.

The Urban District Council has its own schoolattendance committee (until 1902). Teachers attribute some absenteeism to the fact that Leek has a large female labourforce: because the mothers are at work all day in the mills the children, especially the girls, are kept at home to look after brothers and sisters and to run errands.

Waterloo Street is built.

New offices for the Leek and Moorlands Building Society are built at 15 Stockwell Street to the design of J.T. Brealey.

Clerk Bank School closes and the children are moved to Britannia Street.

Haywood Street Smithfield is enlarged by the addition of land in Leonard Street occupied by the town yard.

Vicarage Road, not yet named, is constructed to bypass the steeper Ball Haye Road.

Ball Haye Green Chapel is replaced by a new school in Milk Street.

Sanders Buildings on the corner of Derby Street and Haywood Street is built.

Leek Co-op opens a coal department.

After the boys' building has been remodelled, the girls' and boys' schools at St Luke's are merged, and only the infants are left in Fountain Street.

A chapel is opened in Milk Street at Ball Haye Green.

Another company of the Church Lads' Brigade is formed.

St. Luke's Church organ is installed.

St Edward's Church clock is still the only public clock.

The Quakers meeting is discontinued again.

The Council yard is moved from Leonard Street to Cruso Street.

The Commissioners are replaced by an Urban District Council of twenty-four members with powers covering the same area, 1,459 acres in extent. The area to the south becomes the civil parish of Leek and Lowe.

Members of the Mechanics' Institute consider but reject a proposal to close the Institute and transfer its books to the Nicholson Institute.

At All Saints' Church, an oil painting of the entombment of Christ, now hanging over the vestry door, thought to be of a 17thcentury Venetian School, is given by Thomas Wardle.

Waterloo Mills in Waterloo Street are built by William Broster and Co. with J.G. Smith of Leek as the architect. They resemble Big Mill in general design and in addition are of fireproof construction.

1895 – The Leek and Moorlands Industrial Provident Society Ltd reverts to the old name of Leek and Moorlands Co-operative Society.

The Big Freeze, with sixteen weeks of frost. Rudyard Lake freezes over with ice 18 inches thick. The Leek Volunteers parade on the lake.

Enoch Hill is appointed Secretary of the Leek United Building Society.

George Hill is joined by his sons John and William in the printing business.

The civil parish plus the area to the south becomes the civil parish of Leek and Lowe, renamed Lowe.

Henry Davenport dies.

The Leek and Moorlands Co-operative Society opens a shop on the corner of Picton Street and Britannia Street designed by W. Sugden and Son.

Maude Institute

The plans for remodelling the east side of Market Place arouse opposition and are modified to include only the Butter Market and the new fire station in Stockwell Street.

Leek Highfield Cricket Club is formed. Leek Cricket Club continues at Beggars Lane.

Messrs Brough, Nicholson and Hall take over the Cecily Mills in Cheadle.

The firm of John and Jabez Mathews, bobbin turners, ends its links with the building trade.

C.B. Maude, the vicar from 1887 to 1896, establishes an institute in the former St Edward's School in Clerk Bank, consisting of a working men's club and a young men's union. The schoolhouse at Clerk Bank, plus the land and cottages, is sold. As the Archdeacon of Salop and the Vicar of St Chad's, Shrewsbury, Maude conveys the building to the trustees, and the institute becomes the Maude Church Institute for men and women attending St Edward's. Parishioners subscribe £191 in recognition of Maude's services, and the money is given to the trustees to pay off the mortgage.

Registration of the Wesleyans' room in Haywood Street for the Hallelujah Band Mission is cancelled.

Cookery classes are run by Leek School of Art, Science and Technology at the Hargreaves school, Alsop Street. Those attending include children from local schools.

A large sample of Chardonnet (artificial silk) is received in the town and made up in various ways. It is found to be troublesome and difficult to wind and make up.

Leek Amateur Operatic Society is formed under the patroness the Duchess of Sutherland is formed, usually staging its productions in the Grand Theatre.

The Missions in Angle Street are closed.

The Leek and District Agricultural and Horticultural Society holds its first show on a farm at Belle Vue.

1896 – A new fire station is built at the top of Stockwell Street.

The Butter Market is built and No. 8 Market Place, the saddle shop of George Allen, is removed; the Red Lion is partly rebuilt and enlarged.

The Leek Women's Co-operative Guild is founded. The first meeting is in the Coffee Tavern, and later meetings are held at the William Morris Labour Club on Overton Bank.

Printers in Leek are W.H. Eaton, 6 Derby Street; Clowes and Co., London Road; J. Fogg, Stanley Street; Thomas Grace, Market Place; E. Hallowes, Stockwell Street; Hill Bros, Derby Street; C. Kirkham, Derby Street; M.H. Miller, Market Street

Death of William Challinor, lawyer.

Ernest Worthington dies.

The Christian Men's Club is closed because there are too many rival attractions.

A new company of the Church Lads' Brigade is formed with a room in Shoobridge Street.

The Leek United Permanent Benefit Building Society moves to a new office in St Edward Street.

The Vicar of All Saints', who has hitherto been supported by grants and benefactions, has these stopped when the Ecclesiastical Commissioners grant a stipend of £150 year.

Enoch Hill becomes the secretary of the Leek Building Society. His brothers and father take over the printing business.

Joseph Challinor transfers the patronage of the vicarage of All Saints' to the bishop.

Leek School of Art Science and Technology has an average weekly attendance of 694.

William Haywood, the landlord of the Golden Lion in Church Street, makes mineral water in Naylor's Yard, Clerk Bank.

At All Saints', the processional cross incorporates a latemedieval crucifix from Rhineland, given by Revd. T. Barns.

Alfred Overfield, cabinetmaker, extends his premises to the design of Larner Sugden.

The girls' nonsectarian high school has moved to Russell Street

The Labour Church bearing William Morris's name is established in Leek, chiefly through the influence of Larner Sugden, of the architectural firm of W. Sugden and Son, and leases the Friends' Meeting House at Overton Bank, which then undergoes extensive redecoration by members of the Arts and Crafts movement. The walls are painted red with stencilled tracery designed by Walter Crane. The woodwork is painted translucent green and the windows are provided with blue velvet curtains in Morris fabric. Other furnishings include a blue silk banner painted by Stephen Webb. (None of the decorations or furnishings survive.) The William Morris Labour Church appears to be an amalgamation of a trade union and a religious meeting place and organises regular addresses by notable speakers on humanist, social and religious subjects, which caused local novelist Kineton Parkes to comment that *"a wave of intellectual and semiintellectual activity flooded the town."*

Moses Heapy is producing bottled mineral water in Cross Street

1897 – Jubilee of Queen Victoria

The Butter Market designed by J.T. Brealey of Leek and Hanley opens on the east side of Market Place.

Wardle and Davenport has its own box-making department.

The County Council makes a grant to the girls' nonsectarian High School for science teaching and appoints two representative governors.

West Street Day School is remodelled and improved at the government's insistence.

A clubroom for men and boys of the parish opens south of the church. Almost twothirds of the pupils are artisans, clerks, warehousemen and their children. Pupils included children from local elementary schools sent to school for practical classes.

George Sutton by will leaves £200 for the almswomen.

The Nicholson Institute provides the venue for a course of Cambridge University extension lectures on astronomy.

The Liberal Club for working men opens in Mill Street, known as the Leek Central Liberal Club.

Carved angels are added to the choir stalls of St Luke's Church, in memory of Ernest Worthington, by his brother and sisters.

A plot of land is added to the site of the Cottage Hospital.

The public baths are enlarged.

1898 – General William Booth of the Salvation Army addresses a meeting in the Town Hall.

The Mercantile Bank of Lancashire Ltd opens a branch in Derby Street.

The Liberal Club for working men in Mill Street occupies the former police station in West Street, and is known as the West Street Working Men's Club.

Leek Central Liberal Club moves into the former silk factory in Market Street, redesigned by Larner Sugden.

The *Leek Post* acquires the Leek printing firm of Hill Brothers.

The first Sander and Graf crochet trimming loom in the country is installed in Leek.

A mill is built on east side of Well Street.

Sneyd Street linking Strangman's Walk and Broad Street exists.

The house at the lower end of King Street, dated 1880 and probably built for William Broster, silk manufacturer, is bought as a manse.

The Urban District Council opens the new fire station on Stockwell Street site designed by J.T. Brealey. At same time a steamoperated engine is bought and named the *Queen of the Moorlands*.

The organ at St Edward's Church is replaced by one made by Jardine and Co. of Manchester.

Anglicans no longer walk on the same day as the Nonconformists and the Roman Catholics.

A dispensary still exists.

The Leek Association for the Prosecution of Felons is still meeting.

The infirmary block designed by J.T. Brealey opens.

Moving pictures are shown at the Nicholson Institute by Messrs Stokes and Watson of Manchester.

1899 – Leek's first knitting machine using the latch needle is introduced.

Messrs Brough, Nicholson and Hall introduce the Jacquard looms.

Wardle and Davenport establish a company at Tubize in Belgium for the production of Chardonnet rayon.

Wardle and Davenport becomes a limited company, with a workforce of upwards of 700.

The Urban District Council opens a sewage farm at Barnfields by the southern outfall. Broad irrigation, however, continued north and west of the town until new sewage works were opened.

The foundation stone of Leek Technical Schools is laid by the Duchess of Sutherland on 24 July.

A branch of the Cheque Bank Ltd opens in Shoobridge Street.

Three houses are designed for Spencer Street (later Spencer Avenue).

The Leek and Moorlands Co-operative Society opens a new central premises built in Ashbourne Road, designed by Sugden and Son. They consist of offices, boardroom, hall, grocery and bakery.

William Woodhead sells the Hope Foundry to Mr Hitchcock of Ealing, presumably J.P. Hitchcock, iron and brass founder.

THE TWENTIETH CENTURY

1900 – The girls' nonsectarian high school closes when the mixed high school is opened at the Nicholson Institute. A group of Anglicans immediately open the Leek Church High School for Girls in the Maude Institute, Clerk Bank, employing the staff of the defunct school. The Church High School begins with twenty-five girls and has forty-five by the end of the school year.

A threestoreyed extension is added to the Nicholson Institute to house the High School and the Silk School. It is designed by Sugden and Son with ornamental modelling and lettering by A. Broadbent.

The firm of Hill Brothers, printers, has moved to Haywood Street. It owns the *Leek Post*. It instals the first linotype machine in North Staffordshire.

On 28 July, the Leek Technical School is opened by the Duchess of York (later Queen Mary). The Duke of York lays the foundation stone of the Carr Gymnasium

William Haywood is engaged solely in the production of mineral water.

A new bell for All Saints is cast by Mears and Stainbank of Whitechapel and installed.

The office and warehouse designed by G.H. Chappell is erected in Belle Vue, behind the Big Mill, for Wardle and Davenport.

Matthew Swindells has his spoolmaking business in Queen Street.

There are seven box makers in Leek.

Leek School of Art, Science and Technology has an extension to the Nicholson Institute built partly for the County Silk School. It is promoted by several leading millowners who are irked that Macclesfield has a technical school which provides instruction in silk throwing, spinning and weaving, while all that Leek offers is a class on the theories of silk dyeing.

The mill in Well Street is named the Royal York Mill following a visit by the Duke and Duchess of York.

T. & V. Myatt install machinery to spin silk.

The Urban District Council opens a mixed high school in the Nicholson Institute.

The offices of Leek RDC moved from Challinors and Shaw to Russell Street.

Moses Heapy, producing bottled mineral water in Cross Street, moves his business to Fountain Street.

Travelling theatres visit Leek regularly, including the Bijou Theatre and the Victoria Theatre.

Omnibuses to the railway station run only from the Red Lion and the George.

1901 – Edward VII – Boer War begins

The Carr Gymnasium is opened next to the Nicholson Institute, paid for by William Carr, to designs by Larner Sugden. Carr gives the gymnasium to the Urban District Council.

Death of Hugh Sleigh.

Fred Hill starts a stationery and bookselling business in Derby Street with the print works in Haywood Mill in Haywood Street.

The population of the Urban District is 15,484.

Langford Street and James Street are laid out by James Cornes, a Leek builder, who erects fifty workers' houses there to designs by J.T. Brealey.

Death of Larner Sugden. He is cremated at Manchester, the first person from Leek to be cremated.

The involvement of the friendly societies in Club Day seems to have become only occasional. It is last recorded in this year.

The Leek School of Art, Science and Technology holds practical classes in silk dyeing and weaving at the new school. Despite the pressure and encouragement of employers they arouse little enthusiasm among employees.

The Leek Original Floral and Horticultural Society annual show is still being held at the Blue Ball Inn in Mill Street.

The mixed high school uses the adjoining Carr Gymnasium for extra teaching space as well as for physical training, Although the school is intended mainly for older pupils, with an emphasis on science teaching, it also has preparatory and kindergarten departments.

Three Oddfellows Clubs amalgamate under the name of the Moorlands Lodge.

Large houses are built in Mount Road.

Flat knitting machines are being used.

A fund is established for Morris's Labour Church to continue the addresses and to provide an anniversary lecture in Sugden's honour.

The average attendance in the school in Ball Haye Street is 200 in the mixed school and eighty-three in the infants' school.

The ceiling from No. 8 Market Place is removed to the Carr Gymnasium then being built.

1902 – Elizabeth Wardle dies and the output of the Leek School of Embroidery rapidly declines.

John Robinson dies, leaving Westwood Hall to his wife Helen with a reversion to his three sons. (i.e. his widow has a life interest and the property passes to his sons on her death). Helen Robinson continues to live at the Hall until her death in 1908.

A poultry market is added to the covered market.

The mixed high school in the Nicholson Institute has 149 pupils. The school receives County Council and Government grants, but for some years most of the running costs are paid by a few private benefactors.

Philip Worthington dies. A.J. Worthington and Co. is left in trust for his son, Lancelot, a minor.

The Mechanics' Institute has fewer than 100 members. It survives because of gifts and interestfree loans from wellwishers, and from fundraising activities.

Enoch Hill is appointed secretary to the Halifax Permanent Building Society.

Philip Davenport, the son of George Davenport, dies aged nineteen, in a riding accident at Lowe Hill.

George Davenport engages Thomas Brealey to draw up plans for additions to Foxlowe.

The Rose Society and the British Fern Society amalgamate as the Leek Rose and Fern Society.

John and William Hill, keen photographers, start to produce picture postcards showing local scenes, which is an important side of the business until the late 1920s.

A house in Compton adjoining the church is bought to replace the house in Compton Terrace as the vicarage of All Saints'. It remains the vicarage until 1972.

1903 – Orville and Wilbur Wright fly an aeroplane for the first time

The Council lays out Salisbury Street, Field Street and the west end of High Street on land occupied by the Globe Inn and grounds of a house called The Field and offers thirty-four building plots there for sale.

Isaac Creighton, a bobbin turner, is succeeded by William Creighton, who moves the business to Westwood Terrace.

The Vicar of St Luke's Church opens an institute and recreation room.

Address given in honour of Sugden at the Morris's Labour Church.

The Union Workhouse School is closed down.

The Carr Trust charity becomes effective only after the death of an annuitant, Charles's brother William, who dies in Manchester. He was a businessman who retired to Leek. He leaves his estate of £90,000 for charitable purposes in the town, subject to life interests which expire in 1926, 1939 and 1948.

1904 – High Street is completed, the Globe having been demolished.

Electricity is supplied by the Urban District Council, with a generating station in Cruso Street.

The Leek Amateur Musical Society perform their 100th concert.

The Mercantile Bank of Lancashire Ltd amalgamates with Lancashire and Yorkshire Bank Ltd.

The Hope foundry is being run by J.P. Hitchcock.

Moses Heapy is still producing bottled mineral water in Fountain Street.

George, John and William Hill form George Hill and Sons.

Woodcroft Hall is owned by Marcus Prince, a member of Leek Amateur Operatic Society.

The telephone exchange moves to Haywood Street.

The Leek and Manifold Valley Light Railway is opened to Hulme End. A steampowered omnibus runs from Leek to Waterhouses to connect with it.

The Leek Co-op Society opens the Buxton Road Branch.

1905 – The Post Office is built on the corner of St Edward Street and Strangman's Walk, the east end of which is widened and renamed Strangman Street.

Robert Farrow retires as Sanitary Inspector etc.

The Salvation Army barracks are replaced by a citadel in Union Street.

A bequest of £1,000 from Elizabeth Flint increases the income of the vicar of All Saints; to £210, besides grants from churchwardens, fees and Easter offerings.

Arthur Nicholson is knighted.

The house at the top of the Market Square becomes known as Foxlowe.

A railway line is opened from Leekbrook to join the Leek and Manifold Valley Light Railway at Waterhouses.

Wildt and Co introduce the Brinton knitting machine.

St Luke's mixed school has over 300 children on its books and the infants' school over 200.

The mixed high school in the Nicholson Institute has the curriculum widened in an attempt to attract more pupils. Instead numbers fall and the managers decide to close the school. The County Council persuades them to keep it open.

All Saints' C.E. school has over 400 pupils. The building becomes overcrowded and the managers are forced to cut the numbers.

The last known production by the Leek Philothespian Club.

The charity of Elizabeth Flint of Leek is established by will. The income is to be used for general charitable purposes, including poor relief in Leek. She leaves £500 for the Condlyffe Almshouses.

Spring Gardens, Morley Street and Station Street are laid out.

Wardle and Davenport becomes the first firm in Britain to make artificial silk stockings.

Rudyard Lake Railway station is opened at Cliffe Park.

1906 – The mixed high school in the Nicholson Institute becomes the County High School and the number of pupils begins to increase.

Robert Farrow dies.

Liberals win the election in Leek.

The mission church of St John the Evangelist in Mill Street is under the particular responsibility of an assistant curate at St Edward's.

A separate parish is formed for Longsdon.

William Bromfield becomes a Trade Union Secretary.

The northwest end of Belle Vue is renamed Belle Vue Road and is opened into Mill Street. The route provides access from Mill Street to the railway station avoiding the town centre.

The Club Day procession takes place on the third Saturday in July. The change of date was probably made to dissociate the event from the former Club Day, with its secular entertainments.

The County Council takes over the mixed high school.

1907 – The Cock Lowe is destroyed in the course of the development of the area, but an urn containing a cremation burial of the early or middle Bronze Age is discovered and also a heartshaped carved stone.

The Leek Co-op Society opens the Mill Street and Compton Branches.

Seven of the existing unions unite to form the Leek Textile Federation. Its first and only secretary, William Bromfield, is the secretary of five of the unions. William Stubbs is the secretary of the other two.

Messrs Brough, Nicholson and Hall becomes a private limited company.

At the Mechanics' Institute, the opening of the billiard room enables the institute to survive. Billiards brings in new members and fees from players, and also subsidises the library, which by now consists mainly of popular fiction.

1908 – M. Swindells and Co. are making spools.

George Walker's brewery still in operation.

Westwood Hall is bought by H.L. Johnson, the pottery manufacturer.

The Hope Foundry is run by Churnet Valley Engineering Co., a firm of iron and brass founders.

Mrs Nicholson wipes off all debts of the Leek Highfield Cricket Club and donates two silver cups to be awarded, one for batting and the other for bowling.

There are still some 250 halftimers attending schools, and a suggestion that two schools should be set aside for their exclusive use comes to nothing.

A scheme for the almshouses at the corner of Broad Street and Compton, provides for ten trustees, including the vicars of the three town churches, to choose almswomen for Jolliffe and Ash houses, the vicars with their churchwardens and overseers of Leek and Lowe to choose the women for the Leek houses, and the vicar of St Edward's with appropriate vicars, churchwardens and overseers to choose the women for the houses assigned to the former rural quarters.

The Board of Education considers that the Congregationalists of Union Street school building is no longer adequate.

Death of Joseph Challinor, lawyer.

1909 – **Blériot flies the English Channel**

A separate infants' department is reestablished at the Britannia Street School.

The Mill Street Wesleyan School has an average attendance of 51.

A.J. Worthington and Co. becomes a private limited company.

New firms specialising in knitwear establish themselves in town. One of first is Job White and Sons Ltd, which starts as Trafford and White, a partnership between Herbert Trafford and Job White, working at Victoria Mills in Ball Haye Road.

Death of Sir Thomas Wardle.

The wing of the cottage hospital to designs by W. Sugden and Son is opened. The cost is met by a legacy of £1,000 from Elizabeth Flint and by public subscription. It contains a male and female general ward, each with six beds, and two male and two female accident wards, each with one bed.

Anglicans again take part with others in the Club Day procession.

The Operatic Society changes its name to the Leek Amateur Opera Society.

The building at the back of Mount Pleasant chapel is converted into a social centre called the Wesleyan Institute.

The Grand Theatre and Hippodrome Cinema opens at the corner of High Street and Field Street, at first used chiefly as a music hall.

Hencroft works given up after death of Sir Thomas.

H. Sanders is a printer at Gaunt Passage.

1910 –   George V

Club Day has become known as Leek Sunday School Festival.

The Leek and Moorlands Co-operative Society builds a department store in High Street, designed by R.T. Longden.

The Leek Amateur Opera Society moves the performances from the Town Hall to the Grand Theatre.

St Edward's Church organist is paid £30 a year, mostly from the rent of four plots at the "Organ Land", west of Mount Road, which had been inclosed for that purpose before 1805.

The old church registers from before 1634 have become lost.

Alfred Overfield is a cabinetmaker, and his premises are described as "*one of most complete furnishing establishments in North Staffs*". Sugden designs furniture which Overfield and Co. make under his supervision.

William Bromfield, the secretary of the local textile union, wins the Parliamentary seat for Labour.

The Leek Cattle Market becomes a weekly market.

Morris's Labour Church moves to the Cooperative Society's hall in Ashbourne Road.

The Congregationalists' schools attendance has dropped to 100.

The Grand Theatre in High Street first includes films among its entertainments.

London Road has been renamed Ashbourne Road.

A nine-hole golf course at Cliffe Park (at the north end of Rudyard Lake) is enlarged to eighteen holes.

Vicarage Road is named after the nearby vicarage of St Luke's parish.

The eastern suburb expands as far as Shirburn Road.

1911 –   Trafford and White move to Euston Mills in Wellington Street.

The Thomas Birtles charity still exists and there is a distribution of £2 18s. 4d. made in two-shilling doles.

Shirley Street is built.

The almshouses at the corner of Broad Street and Compton are restored. The work involves raising the roof by 2 feet and extending the back walls.

The almshouses in StratforduponAvon, St Joseph's Homestead, are founded by Agnes and Rose Edith CarrSmith, the nieces of William Carr of Leek (d. 1903). Christian widows or spinsters resident in the area of the former Leek Urban District are eligible to apply for a place.

A rollerskating rink at the corner of High Street and Salisbury Street is converted to a cinema, known at first as the Salisbury Electric Picture Palace.

The Leek and Moorlands Co-op Society opens the Emporium in High Street.

The bowling green is opened in Beggars Lane and used by Leek Bowling Club.

Sir Arthur Nicholson presents a new pavilion to the Leek Highfield Cricket Club.

General William Booth of the Salvation Army addresses a meeting in the Town Hall.

1912 – **Sinking of *Titanic***

The Salvation Army citadel in Union Street is replaced by a hall in Ball Haye Road.

Trafford and White moves to Compton Mills by exchange with Henry Bermingham and Son.

The Pride of the Moorlands Lodge of the Order of the Sisters is affiliated to the Independent Order of Oddfellows (Manchester Unity).

Alsop Street school has 100 on the roll.

M. Swindells and Co. has a second works at Portland Mills and has switched to the production of bobbins.

The Hope Foundry has been renamed the Churnet Foundry.

Mercerised cotton (cotton that has been treated to make it look like silk) is being produced in Leek.

George Davenport dies aged 59, leaving £105,403.

Spearings, cheese factors, are at 24 Market Place.

The *Leek Post* is published by Hill Bros (Leek) Ltd, 79 Haywood Street. The *Leek Times* is published in Pickwood Road by the North Stafford Newspaper Co.

No. 1 Stockwell Street (the White Hart) is occupied by H.J. Gaddman and Co., yarn merchants.

A 14th century silvergilt North German chalice and silver Swiss chalice dated 1641 is given to St Edward's Church by Mrs Barron (née Gaunt).

The Leek branch of the Charity Organization Society still exists.

At the Leek School of Art, Science and Technology, the number of pupils on the register is twenty-five in the weaving classes and seven in the dyeing classes.

Seven firms are engaged in Leek in silk dyeing.

1913 – Renewed government pressure for improvements to the building leads to the closure of schools in Ball Haye Street.

William Spooner Brough of Leek (d. 1917) establishes a charity for the relief in kind of the poor of Leek.

There is a successful strike in the textile trade.

On 23 April, King George V and Queen Mary come to Leek and visit Wardle's Dye Works, Belle Vue, Garden Street, Westwood Road, Bangate Street, Cruso Street, Broad Street, St Edward Street, Sheepmarket, Market Place, Derby Street, Ashbourne Road, Messrs Brough, Nicholson and Hall in Cross Street, Market Street, the Town Hall, Stockwell Street, Church Street, Belle Vue and Highfield Hall.

W.S. Brough gives the Urban District Council 10½ acres of his Ball Haye Hall estate for use as a public park. Because of the First World War the conversion is postponed.

Leek Amateur Musical Society still exists.

The Abbey View Tennis Club is formed with courts on part of the Ball Haye Hall estate given that year for Brough Park.

The Leek and District Manufacturers' and Dyers' Association is formed. The first president is Sir Arthur Nicholson, who holds office until 1929.

Leek is the only place in the administrative county where children attend school halftime.

Congregationalists of Union Street close.

The Mill Street Wesleyan School is closed, but the building continues in use as a chapel.

1914 – First World War begins

William Davis replaces Herbert Trafford at Job White & Co.

Additional accommodation is added to the County High School at the Nicholson Institute.

Leek's first council school is built.

The Salvation Army move to a hall in Ford Street.

The children stop begging for soul cakes on All Saints' Day.

St Luke's Tennis Club exists.

Leek's first council school is opened in East Street with accommodation for 100 infants and 354 older children. Two silk manufacturers, John Hall and Sir Arthur Nicholson, paid half of the cost of building the infants' school.

The house known as The Field is used as a registration centre for those enlisting during the First World War (and later becomes Leek National Reserve Club).

George Davenport's furniture is offered for sale but withdrawn.

1915 – The Grand Theatre is principally used as a cinema. It is also used for performances by visiting professional companies, and local amateur societies' presentations are occasionally given there.

Lieutenant B.L. Nicholson is killed in action.

Foxlowe is used as a Red Cross Hospital.

1914 ~ Leek Troop

1916 – Father Alfred Spurling, who was the priest at Leek in 1884, is appointed the private chamberlain to the Pope. In 1923 he is created Monsignor.

Haworths occupies 1 Stockwell Street and Gadman is at No. 3.

Ralph Mountfort is still engaged in grocery and twine manufacture.

Leek United Permanent Benefit Building Society moves to premises in St Edward Street.

The Hope Foundry is still running, having added production of machine tools to its activities.

1917 – Russian Revolution begins

Death of William Spooner Brough.

On 14 October the Federation of Textile Unions offers to buy Foxlowe for £3,000.

1918 – William Bromfield is elected as Labour MP for the Leek division, as well as secretary of the new union. Foxlowe, the former home of the Cruso family in Church Street, becomes the union's headquarters. This is of great symbolic importance.

Ball Haye Domestic Subjects Centre, at which children from Leek are schools taught cookery, laundry and household care, is opened.

Parr's Banking Co. Ltd merges with London and Westminster Bank Ltd to form London County Westminster and Parr's Bank Ltd.

White and Davis becomes a private limited company

1919 – Lady Astor is the first woman to take her seat as an MP

The two cricket clubs reunite as the Leek Cricket Club, using the Highfield ground for matches and Beggars Lane for practice.

Leek is omitted from the County Council's plans for reorganising the elementary schools apparently because "*the denominational difficulty would be great*".

The Earl of Macclesfield sells the Grammar School building.

The Leek Church High School for girls becomes a maintained County High School for girls with sixty-six pupils.

Motor buses running to Hanley, Ashbourne, Cheadle and Buxton are introduced.

Seven unions amalgamate to form the Amalgamated Society of Textile Workers and Kindred Trades. The Twisters' Union remains separate.

The Leek United Permanent Benefit Building Society changes its name to the Leek United and Midlands Building Society.

The recreation ground at Ball Haye Green is laid out as a war memorial.

1920 – July fairs have changed to the first and last Wednesdays of that month.

A.J. Worthington and Co. Ltd of Portland Mills in Portland Street and Queen Street is one of the larger firms in Leek, with a workforce of 400.

The first houses provided by the Urban District Council consist of twelve wooden huts erected in Junction Road on part of Barnfields Farm, later the site of the cattle market. Faced with a housing shortage, the council buys the huts from the government, transports them, and converts them into temporary dwellings. The council's first permanent estate of 24 acres is the Abbottsville estate west of Abbotts Road, where 258 houses are built between 1920 and 1924.

Williams Deacon's Bank opens a branch in Derby Street.

Westwood Hall, the home of H.J. Johnson, plus fourteen acres of land, is sold to Staffordshire County Council, which turns it into a school.

Brough Nicholson and Hall Ltd becomes one of the largest mills with premises covering several acres and employing 2,000.

A firm of pump manufacturers, Moorlands Engineering Co. Ltd, opens works by the canal wharf.

The mill in Belle Vue is enlarged to the design of R.T. Longden.

Alsop Street School has forty-seven on the roll.

Additional accommodation is added to the County High School at the Nicholson Institute.

Leek Cricket Club buys the Beggars Lane site.

Wardle and Davenport conveys its manufacture of mercerised cotton along with the Big Mill to PeriLusta Ltd.

Fred Hill buys three cottages in Getliffe Yard off Derby Street, opposite his shop and converts them into print works.

Burton Street is built.

DieuLacresse Masonic Lodge is formed.

Messrs Brough, Nicholson and Hall have a dyeworks at Bridge End.

1921 – Population of Leek and Lowe is 16,663.

Leek Cripples' Aid Society is formed. It works at first in the Ball Haye Street schools and the Memorial Hospital.

Leek Central Liberal Club ceases to act politically.

Leek has a motor ambulance for noninfectious and accident cases and a horse-drawn vehicle for infectious cases.

Leek Church High School for girls is closed.

Westwood Hall is opened as a girls' high school. It takes older girls from the mixed Leek County High School at the Nicholson Institute and older pupils from the Church High School for girls at the Maude Institute, with the Nicholson Institute housing the boys' high school and the mixed preparatory department.

Alsop Street school is closed.

St. Luke's Tennis Club existed.

Wardles becomes a private limited company.

Land given to the Urban District Council by W.S. Brough at Ball Haye Green is extended by another 8½ acres given by Joseph Tatton.

1922 – **BBC begins broadcasting on 2LO**

Leek Mineral Water Co. has works in London Street.

Fred Adams starts his buttermaking business at Springfield Farm.

The Majestic cinema occupies the former Temperance Hall in Union Street.

John and Jabez Mathews, bobbin turners, are still in business.

There are still halftimers in Leek schools when such attendance is brought to an end nationally.

George Hill, printer, dies.

Only a few Leek firms sell and overhaul mill machinery.

Kniveden Quarry is again worked.

Sneyd Engineering Co. Ltd is in existence.

1923 – Fred Adams installs a cold store at Springfield Farm.

The bowling green is opened in Brough Park.

The Westwood Golf Club on the north side of Newcastle Road near Wallbridge is formed, at first for artisans.

W.H. White and Sons of Old Bank Mill and Ball Haye Road begin.

Leek Golf Club moves to a course on the west side of Cheddleton Road, with a clubhouse designed by Longden and Venables.

The land given by W.S. Brough is called "Brough Park".

1924 – Work begins on the Nicholson War Memorial, on the open space at the end of Derby Street then being used as part of the cattle market. The Memorial is a clock tower of white Portland stone designed by Thomas Worthington and Sons of Manchester, and given by Sir Arthur and Lady Nicholson, whose son Lt. B.L. Nicholson died in action in 1915.

The Mechanics' Institute appeals for new members and is apologetic about the old-fashioned word "*mechanics*" while, at the same time, finding it necessary to assure working people that they would be welcome.

William Davis resigns from Trafford and White.

Brough Park is officially opened and the bandstand built.

The Challinor Fountain is moved to Brough Park.

The Salisbury Electric Picture Palace is known as the Palace Picture Theatre.

Wardle and Davenport's various factories cover 15 acres and employ 2,500 people. The Big Mill in the meantime is transferred to a separate company for the production of mercerised cotton.

Ralph Mountfort is involved in grocery only, having dropped rope and twine manufacture.

A motor fire engine is bought, named *Wilson* after the chairman of the fire brigade committee. The steam engine is retained.

Alfred Overfield, cabinetmaker, ceases business.

The Spiritualists hold services in the Friends' Meeting House at Overton Bank.

Leek and Moorlands Building Society premises in Stockwell Street are extended.

A nineacre estate in Nab Hill Avenue and Hillswood Avenue is built as a private initiative by Solomon Bowcock, the secretary of Leek United and Midlands Building Society, to provide houses for people of moderate means. The houses are designed by Longden and Venables.

Services to the railway station from the Red Lion and George have been reduced to market day (Wednesday) only.

The hospital convalescent committee presents a new motor ambulance to the town, and the existing ambulance is transferred to infectious cases.

Trafford and White is renamed Job White and Sons Ltd.

Wardle and Davenport build a factory in Hillswood Avenue specially for the production of boxes.

Leek Rugby Union Football Club is formed.

1925 – Glebeville estate off Junction Road adjoining Sandon Road (later Sandon Street) has begun by private development.

By will, R.S. Milner establishes a general educational charity for Leek Urban District. (The compiler of these articles was not the only child to benefit from this charity when he first went to the Leek High School in 1953.) The charity is administered by Messrs Challinor and Shaw, Solicitors, of 10 Derby Street.

The Council builds forty-six houses on the south side of town. Most of them are in Glebeville off Junction Road on 2½ acres of glebe bought from the trustees of All Saints' church, but some on the remainder of Barnfields Farm.

The telephone exchange moves to the Post Office.

There only fifty-eight privies in the area, twenty-eight of them in outlying rural areas without sewers.

The Abbotts Road Council Estate is extended north to Novi Lane with another seventy-two houses in 1925 and 1926.

The Adams family starts its butter business and becomes one of the first companies in the country to introduce prepacked butter.

The War Memorial Tower is dedicated.

The new presbytery is completed north of St Edward's Church.

The western end of Belle Vue Mill is rebuilt as an office block, to designs by Longden. Wardle and Davenport takes over several smaller concerns, including the dyeworks at Bridge End belonging to William Hammersley and Co.

The Leek and Moorlands Co-operative Society bakery is replaced by one in Strangman Street to designs by Longden and Venables.

Fred Hill, printers, at Christmas issues *Leek News*, an advertising journal which is delivered free to every household in Leek. It continues every year until 1938.

1926 – General Strike – Queen Elizabeth II born

The Congregational Manse in King Street becomes a hall for the town's Freemasons.

Ball Haye Green Working Men's Institute, designed by Wilfred Ingram, is built in Ball Haye Green Road opposite Prince Street, and is known as Ball Haye Green Working Men's Club.

Leek Orchestral Society disbands, for lack of support.

The Ball Haye Domestic Subjects Centre is still going strong.

Two more bells are added at St Edward's Church, cast by Gillett and Johnson of Croydon.

A number of large houses, to designs by Longden and Venables, are built at Big Birchall.

Barclays Bank opens a branch in Derby Street.

1927 – Leek Cripples' Aid Society is opened with a clinic in Salisbury Street designed by Longden and Venables.

St Luke's church organ is moved from the north aisle into the chancel, and a wooden chancel screen is erected in memory of William Challinor (d. 1926) and his daughter Mary Watson.

At the mission church of St John the Evangelist in Mill Street, a detached recreation room is built.

A new Amateur Dramatic Society is formed.

An operatic society is established at All Saints' Church.

East Street Primary School is extended.

Midland Bank opens its branch in Derby Street.

Nab Hill Avenue and Hillswood Avenue are completed.

The firm becomes Joshua Wardle Ltd.

Leek Alexandra Football Club still exists.

The last performance of Leek Amateur Opera Society.

1928 – At the west end of the town, 114 houses are built in Station Street, The Walks and Morley Street.

The farmhouse at Big Birchall is still standing but is later demolished.

The service to the railway station from the Red Lion and the George ceases.

A bus service is introduced to Butterton.

The Lancashire and Yorkshire Bank Ltd is taken over by Martins Bank Ltd.

The council houses are completed in Station Street.

The first charitable disbursement from the Carr Trust is made, when the beneficiaries are the almshouses established by his sister Isabella Carr, the cottage hospital, the cripples' clinic and the Cruso Nursing Association.

The Mechanics' Institute's trustees decide that it no longer has any useful function.

The new telephone exchange is opened in the post office yard in Strangman Street.

Enoch Hill is knighted.

Leek Park Bowling Club is formed, and uses the greens in Brough Park.

William Haywood is still engaged in the production of mineral water.

1929 – The Mechanics' Institute closes.

The bridge at Wallbridge is widened.

Fred Adams' son, another Fred, joins the firm.

Joshua Wardle Ltd builds a second works, adjoining the first, to designs by Longden and Venables, which includes the site of the Travellers' Rest inn, which was rebuilt on the opposite side of Cheddleton Road, also to the design of Longden and Venables.

The charity of W.S. Brough (see 1913) still exists but no later record can be found.

Part of the income from the Carr Trust is used to open a soup kitchen for schoolchildren in the Butter Market.

1930 – St Luke's Church parish hall is opened in the Organ Ground, the lane between Shirburn Road and Springfield Road, on a site given by the Challinor family in memory of William Challinor (d. 1926). The building becomes an annexe to the primary school in East Street in 1954. (The compiler attended a nursery school in this building in 1945/6.)

Edward Bostock includes Leek in what proves to be Wombwell's Menagerie's last tour.

St. John's mixed and infants' school has 202 on the roll.

Trotters are still employed by twisters.

Building continues north of Novi Lane on 29 acres at Haregate, where 104 houses are built.

The cemetery is again extended.

The County Council becomes the local Education Authority.

Two shops (Birch and Bradley) are demolished at the top left of the Market Place.

F.W. Woolworths alter the ground level of their building (bottom of Market Place).

Whittles mill in Strangman Street ceases to be steampowered.

The residential areas are extended by the building of council estates, Abbottsville and Haregate estates. Prince Street is extended from Ball Haye Green to Buxton Road as part of Abbottsville estate.

The Britannia Street school has 454 on the roll.

The mission church in Ball Haye Green is known as St Paul's.

West Street day school has 440 on the books.

St Mary's mixed and infants' school has 194 on its books.

All Saints' C.E. school has 361 on roll.

The day school in Pump Street is a mixed and infants' school with 142 on its books. It is agreed that it should become a junior school in the general reorganisation of Leek schools.

1931 – Electricity supply is extended to Birchall.

Pentecostalists first meet in Leek, using the Congregationalists' Hall in Russell Street before moving to premises in Globe Passage off High Street.

Conservatives win the Leek election.

The bridge across the River Churnet on the Congleton Road is widened on both sides.

The population of Leek and Lowe is 18,567.

The Black's Head inn is converted into a "*fancy bazaar*" by F.W. Woolworth and Co. Ltd.

Compton becomes a junior mixed and infants' school.

Britannia Street School becomes a senior mixed school.

St Mary's mixed and infants' school becomes a junior school.

St Luke's mixed school becomes a junior school, with 256 on its books, Thereafter numbers dwindle in both junior and infants' schools.

St. John's C.E. School, Mill Street becomes a junior school.

West Street becomes a junior school, and numbers are reduced as the building is inadequate.

Eight elementary schools in town are reorganised as junior and senior schools. Over the next few years the schools in the neighbouring villages become junior schools, the older children being brought into Leek by bus.

William Bromfield stands down as Labour MP for Leek.

On 26 September, Bostock and Wombwell's menagerie on its final tour calls at Market Place, Leek.

In July, Prince George visits Brough, Nicholson and Hall.

East Street School becomes a senior school, with 334 on the roll

Wakes Monday is still a school holiday.

The Council opens the reservoir at Kniveden mainly to supply the Ashbourne Road area.

1932 – The Quakers have another revival, but the Friends have to meet in private houses.

Products which made use of the Leek School of Embroidery designs continue to be sold in the St Edward Street shop until it closes.

In Leekfrith, the Urban District Council buys the freehold of the springs at Upper Hulme before the lease expires.

Alterations to the Britannia Street School provide additional classrooms.

Spearings, cheese factors, move to 13 Stockwell Street.

Bus services are introduced to Macclesfield and Manchester and also to Calton and Longnor.

1933 – A sewage farm is established at Wallbridge.

The Masonic Hall is extended.

Hubert Newton is appointed the secretary of Leek and Moorlands Building Society at the age of twenty-nine. He is later to be the general manager, the managing director, the chairman, and the president.

1934 – The Emmanuel Baptist Church in Rosebank Street is registered for Old Baptists.

Traffic on the canal has never been heavy, and the transport of coal now ceases completely.

The Manifold Valley Light Railway closes.

At Adams Dairies (Wholesale) a printing department is added to print the firm's butter wrappers and labels for customers.

Hill Brothers take over the *Leek Times*, and amalgamates it with the *Leek Post* as the *Leek Post and Times*.

New sewage works are opened at Leekbrook.

The Urban District is enlarged to 4,315 acres by the addition of Lowe parish and parts of parishes of Cheddleton, Leekfrith, Longsdon and Tittesworth, with four wards created.

1935 – Although Morris's Labour Church has ceased holding religious services, the church is still active politically.

Two societies, the Leek Choral Society and Leek Orchestral Society, give joint concerts.

The Spiritualists run a Sunday school at Overton Bank.

William Bromfield regains the Parliamentary seat for Labour.

Another 156 houses are built at Haregate north of Novi Lane to rehouse the people displaced by slum clearance.

The Council builds a pumping station at Poolend in Leekfrith linked to the Mount Road and Kniveden reservoirs.

Passenger services are withdrawn from the Leekbrook to Waterhouses railway line.

Beresford Memorial C.E. (Aided) First School, St Paul's School, Novi Lane, is opened as a junior mixed school with 101 on the roll.

The mission in the Alsop Street school is closed.

1936 – Leek and Moorlands Building Society replace their premises with New Stockwell House, built on the site of Stockwell House to the design of Briggs and Thornely of Liverpool.

The covered market is again extended.

The hall at the corner of Salisbury Street and Strangman Street is registered for the Salvation Army.

In Leek there are eleven firms involved in silk dyeing.

The company is renamed A.J. Worthington and Co. (Leek) Ltd.

The northern Rudyard Lake Railway station name is changed to Cliffe Park.

The William Morris Labour Church surrenders the lease of the Quaker Meeting House on Overton Bank.

1937 – Ginger beer production by Richard Massey in Leonard Street ends.

Several large houses are built on Buxton Road between Abbotts Road and Novi Lane.

The Quakers resume their Leek meetings.

There are five firms of textile engineers in the town.

Leek School of Art, Science and Technology continues as the County School of Hosiery Manufacture and Dyeing.

A private estate has been built west of Newcastle Road over the site and grounds of Woodcroft and over the grounds of Woodcroft Grange, another late 19thcentury house.

The Leek County Senior School, Springfield Road (later the Milner County Secondary Modern School for Girls and Mountside County Secondary Modern School for Boys) opens, with 483 on the roll.

The Urban District Council buys 24 acres at Birchall Dale on the west side of Cheddleton Road. The playing fields are laid out for hire to local clubs.

St Mary's infants' school moves to new buildings in Cruso Street, and is named Monsignor A.M. Sperling Memorial School after a priest who has served at Leek from 1884 to 1923.

The senior school in East Street moves to new buildings in Springfield Road. The infants' school has 150 children divided among three infant classes and a junior class, and expands into the vacated premises and becomes a full primary school.

1938 – The Leek and Moorlands Building Society takes over the Longton Mutual Permanent Benefit Building Society.

Westwood County First School, Westwood Road, opens.

The County High School at the Nicholson Institute is overcrowded and ninety boys have to be taught elsewhere in town.

The hospital on the west side of Ashbourne Road is taken over by Newcastle and District Joint Hospital Board.

The extension of Wardle's Churnet Works begins.

The mission church of St John the Evangelist in Mill Street school is closed, but the building continues in use as a mission church.

The managers propose the closure of West Street day school because they cannot afford the improvements required. The outbreak of the Second World War foils plans for alternative accommodation.

Control of the School of Art, Science and Technology passes from the Urban District Council to the County Council.

Houses are built in Beggars Lane.

1939 – Second World War

The Hargreaves School is being used as a practical instruction centre and clinic for schoolchildren.

A new building at the Britannia Street school, Milward Hall, is added in Salisbury

Street. The adjoining school comprises housecraft and handicraft rooms and an assembly hall which is also used as a gymnasium.

The use of the canal to carry tar from Milton ceases.

The boys' school moves to the still unfinished building in Westwood Road. The preparatory department is divided. Boys under eight and girls remain at the Nicholson Institute and become the responsibility of Westwood Hall Girls' High School. The older boys go to Westwood Road.

The Twisters Union is dissolved

1940 – M. Swindells and Co. are still in business making bobbins in Portland Street.

The day school in Pump Street becomes an infants' school.

The Boys' High School in Westwood Road is completed and the part of Nicholson Institute vacated by the high school is used from 1940 to 1943 by the boys of Parmiter's School, evacuated from the East End of London.

There are ten box makers in Leek, including G.H. Plant and Sons.

The second son, John Adams, joins the butter makers partnership, which becomes a private company called Adams Butter Ltd.

Many children are evacuated to Leek, mainly from Manchester, Liverpool, London and Essex.

The Milner County Secondary Modern School for Girls and Mountside County Secondary Modern School for Boys is divided into Leek County Senior School (Boys) and Leek County Senior School (Girls).

1941 – Bethesda Chapel at corner of Ball Haye Street and Queen Street is closed.

In March, a German bomber unloads its bombs on the town, killing one man and damaging several buildings.

A German bomber, hit during a raid on Liverpool, comes down on the Roches.

1942 – The former Ball Haye Street schools are converted into a British restaurant.

The Pentecostalists move to Strangman Street.

The Jehovah's Witnesses meet in a room in Globe Passage off High Street.

William Bromfield retires from the Trade Union movement.

St Luke's church hall is fitted up as a day nursery for forty children aged from two to five in order to free their mothers for work.

1943 – The two St Luke's schools are merged to form a junior and infants' school with 130 Leek children and twelve evacuees on its books.

On the southwest tower column of St Luke's Church is a crucifix thought to be 16thcentury Spanish and given in memory of W.G. Keyworth, the vicar from 1921 to 1941.

Hundreds of American soldiers arrive, based at Blackshaw Moor with a camp for officers in the grounds of Ball Haye Hall, and another for other ranks at Hencroft off the Abbey Green Road.

Williams Deacon's Bank in Derby Street closes.

The section of the railway between Cauldon and Waterhouses is closed.

John and William Hill, printers, retire, selling the business to John Myatt.

East Street Primary School has 325 on the roll and becomes the town's largest primary school.

1944 – Britannia Street School becomes an aided secondary modern school under the 1944 Education Act.

The US troops leave on or after D-Day.

Under the 1944 Act, the Boys' High School in Westwood Road becomes a grammar school.

The Jehovah's Witnesses meet in a room in King Street.

A number of RAF aircraft crash in the Leek area during the war, on the Roches, Hen Cloud and Morridge. Most of them are on training exercises.

Brindley's mill closes.

The Leek County Senior School (Boys) and Leek County Senior School (Girls) become secondary modern schools under the 1944 Act.

1945 – End of the war

House building resumes.

Harold Davies wins the election for Labour.

Two earlier portions of the covered market are adapted to provide fixed lockup stalls.

The day school in Pump Street closes. The staff and pupils are transferred to Beresford Memorial school, Novi Lane. The building continues in use as a mission church.

1945 - VE Day

1946 – Tom Birch JP dies aged 67.

Herbert Lisle is appointed the Secretary of the Trade Union Movement.

During the Second World War numbers decline at St Paul's School, Novi Lane. Staff and pupils of St Luke's infants' school at Ball Haye Green are transferred to Novi Lane to create a junior mixed and infants' school with 128 on the roll.

Slum clearance resumes, having been Discontinued during the Second World War.

Messrs Brough, Nicholson and Hall become a public company.

Leek Rugby Union Football Club is revived, playing on the ground at Birchall Dale.

1947 – The Conservative Association is dissolved.

A.J. Worthington and Co. take over several firms after the Second World War.

With closure of the small country schools after the War, many younger children are brought into Leek. The harsh moorland winter causes problems with transport.

1948 – The Haregate estate is purchased by the Council for future council houses to be built.

The soup kitchen supported by charity in Mill Street is closed.

The Boys' High School in Westwood Road has 351 pupils.

Leek Town FC moves to its present ground in Macclesfield Road.

Ball Haye Green Football Club moves to its present ground behind Ball Haye Green Working Men's Club.

Part of Brindley's Mill is demolished for road widening.

St Luke's Players are in existence.

Leek and District Arts Club is founded with support from the Urban District Council and the Arts Council of Great Britain. The UDC converts the museum in the Nicholson Institute into a meeting and concert room for the club.

The workhouse buildings pass to StokeonTrent Hospital Management Committee and become the Moorlands Hospital.

1949 – Wardles becomes a public company.

The West Street day school takes on controlled status and shortly afterwards is renamed the Mount Methodist School.

Two bronze tablets are unveiled at the Monument recording the names of those killed during the Second World War.

The former Bethesda Chapel at the bottom of Queen Street is taken over by the former Primitive Methodist congregation from Fountain Street. The Fountain Street building is used for various purposes.

East Street Primary School has over 400 on roll.

The Methodist Chapel in Fountain Street closes.

The Arts Club room at the Nicholson Institute is opened as an arts centre, one of first six in the country to be recognised by the Arts Council.

1950 – Boys' High School preparatory department is closed.

The Britannia Street School has 290 on the roll. The Government inspector remarks unfavourably on the school's cramped towncentre site and considers that the buildings are inadequate.

Westwood Hall Girls' High School preparatory school department is closed.

Leek remains an industrial town concerned mainly with textiles, but new fibres, natural and manmade, become predominant.

The Benevolent Burial Society has become a general insurance society known as the Leek Assurance Collecting Society, with an office in Russell Street.

William Bromfield dies aged 82.

1951 – The population of Leek and Lowe is 19,356.

The British Restaurant at the Primitive Methodist Chapel in Fountain Street, having moved from the Ball Haye School in 1949, is closed.

Jehovah's Witnesses meet in a room in Barngate Street.

Leek mill holiday is taken on first Monday in October.

1954 – The land on the west side of Ashbourne Road is closed and sold to the Urban District Council for conversion into dwellings. The council builds old people's bungalows in the garden.

The East Street Primary School numbers continue to grow. St Luke's church hall is hired to provide extra accommodation.

Westwood Road junior mixed and infants' council school changes its name and the word "Road" is gradually dropped from its title

The last burial at the Quaker Meeting House take place.

1955 – Barclays Bank moves to new premises in Derby Street.

The School of Art, Science and Technology is divided into the College of Further Education and the School of Art and Crafts, both housed at the Nicholson Institute.

Large council estates have been built at Haregate and Selbourne Road.

The Leek and District Agricultural and Horticultural Society Show lapses.

A further 557 houses and flats have been provided. They included thirty more in Novi Lane and Abbotts Road, 248 on the Compton estate including nine flats in the adapted Compton House, and 268 on Haregate estate. A site of 3½ acres has also been acquired in Westwood Heath Road.

Leek County Senior Girls' School is renamed the Milner school after R.S. Milner, the founder of a local educational charity.

Leek remains the centre of the silk sewing thread trade in 1950s, although the number of firms engaged in silk production is dwindling.

Most of the streets are still lit by gas, and the Council is planning systematic conversion to electricity.

1956 – The town ambulances are kept in the town yard in Cruso Street.

The private Westwood estate is begun.

Jehovah's Witnesses meet in a room in Ball Haye Street.

Messrs Brough, Nicholson and Hall sell Bridge End dye-works to Sir Thomas and Arthur Wardle Ltd.

Having bought Brough, Nicholson and Hall's Bridge End dye-works, Wardles establishes its subsidiary, Leek Chemicals Ltd, there.

The side galleries are removed at St Edward's Church.

1957 – A separate infants' school is opened in Whitfield Street.

The canal is abandoned under an Act of 1944 and the stretch north of the River Churnet aqueduct is bought by the Leek Urban District Council and later filled in. It is now the site of part of Barnfields industrial estate.

An ambulance station is opened in Haregate Road.

1958 – Fred Hill retires from the printing business, and Albert Hughes, his brother-inlaw, takes over the business.

Leek Amateur Dramatic Society gives its last production.

East Street Primary School has over 500 on the roll.

West Street day school has 300 on the books.

The Leekensian Amateur Operatic Society is formed.

Spiritualists cease meetings at Overton Bank.

Most of the cottages in Mill Street are demolished.

1959 – There are 476 on the roll at Milner School and the building is extended, with the boys' school renamed the Mountside School.

1960 – Barclays Bank moves to other premises on Haywood Street.

The cattle market is transferred to a sevenacre site off Junction Road. The bus station and the shopping precinct are built on the Haywood Street site.

The May fair, having been held on the Haywood Street Smithfield, is also transferred to the new Smithfield.

Moorlands Engineering Co. Ltd closes its works by the canal wharf, leaving only one foundry in Leek, in Sneyd Street belonging to Sneyd Engineering.

Rail passenger services between Leek and Stoke and between Leek and Macclesfield cease.

The Leekensian Amateur Operatic Society performs in the Grand Theatre.

1961 – The population of Leek and Lowe is 19,182.

The Magistrates' Court moves to part of the Methodist Sunday School building in Regent Street.

An operatic society is established at All Saints' Church called the All Saints' Amateur Operatic Society.

Slum clearance continues: 283 dwellings have been demolished out of 450 scheduled for demolition.

The Majestic cinema is gutted by fire and destroyed.

Albert Hughes dies. His widow Hannah carries on the printing business in partnership with Ray Poole, who has been Hughes's assistant.

1962 – Work begins on the bus station and shopping centre on the site of the former cattle market in Haywood Street.

The Palace cinema, now called the Regal, becomes a bingo hall.

The District Bank becomes a subsidiary of National Provincial Bank Ltd.

Job White and Sons becomes a public company.

Numbers at St Luke's School recovered in the 1950s, but from the early 1960s there are never more than 100 on the books.

Messrs Brough, Nicholson and Hall begin a fouryear modernisation programme, with activities concentrated in Cross Street and at Cheadle. The knitting department is transferred to Job White and Sons Ltd of Compton Mills, which takes over the London and York mills.

There are some small engineering works in Leek which are ancillary to the textile trade.

Leek and District Agricultural and Horticultural Society Show is revived as an annual event at Birchall.

A Saturday general market is introduced.

East Street Primary School is deemed to be overcrowded.

There are fewer than 150 pupils at All Saints' C.E. school. The managers are finding it increasingly difficult to maintain the building to the required standards and parents are sending their children elsewhere.

Brassington and Sons (Leek) Ltd, with its works in Cornhill Street, is the only firm of bobbin manufacturers in town.

1963 – The Primitive Methodist Chapel at Bethesda is closed again, and used for commercial purposes.

Several of the larger textile firms have their own box-making departments, but there also six independent box manufacturers.

A J. Worthington (Holdings) Ltd. consists of six companies.

At All Saints', a silver chalice and paten dated 1569 are given under the will of Gilbert Tatton.

The bus station is opened on the former cattle market in Haywood Street.

Wallbridge Park is begun.

A junior training centre is established by the County Council in Springfield Road.

1964 – The Mount Road reservoir is enlarged.

The Moorlands Lodge Oddfellows Club closes.

The gasworks ceases production.

The new Post Office is opened further north in St Edward Street.

Job White and Sons is one of the largest manufacturers of knitted headwear in the country, employing some 600 people, over half at Compton and the rest at London and York mills, which it has acquired from Brough Nicholson and Hall, and at Hope Mill in Macclesfield Road.

The Jehovah's Witnesses meeting cease.

The wrapper and box division of Adams Butter Ltd is opened in the former silk mill in Queen Street, and an office block is built on the site adjoining the main factory.

The railway line north from Leek is closed for freight.

Compton Mills is burnt down.

A class for children with special educational needs is housed in part of Mount School, West Street.

Martins Bank Ltd moves to the former Savings Bank building on the corner of Derby Street and Russell Street.

Lloyds Bank opens its branch in the Smithfield Centre in Haywood Street.

1965 – St Luke's Tennis Club closes.

Leek Federation of Local Trades Unions achieves new importance when the National Silk Workers' and Textile Trades Association is merged with it.

Comprehensive secondary education is introduced.

Passenger rail services between Leek and Uttoxeter cease.

Compton Mill is reopened.

Westwood Hall High School merges with the newly built St Edward's C.E. (Aided) Secondary School in Westwood Park Avenue to form a mixed comprehensive, Westwood County High School.

Leek and Moorlands Building Society merges with Westbourne Park Building Society, to become the sixth largest building society in the country. It is renamed Leek and Westbourne.

Britannia Street School closes. The pupils are transferred to a secondary school built by the governors in Westwood Park Road and opened that year as part of the new comprehensive Westwood High School. The Britannia Street building and Milward Hall are sold.

The Boys' High School in Westwood Road merges with the two secondary modern schools in Springfield Road – Milner and Mountside – to form a mixed comprehensive secondary school on two sites. The Westwood Road building becomes the new school's Warrington Hall, named after T.C. Warrington, headmaster of the high school from 1900 to 1934.

All Saints' C.E. school moves into new buildings further south in Cheadle Road.

The Milner and Mountside schools become Milner Hall and Mountside Hall of the mixed comprehensive Leek High School.

The completion of the new St Edward's C.E. (Aided) Secondary School in Westwood Park Avenue to replace the parish church schools in Britannia Street coincides with the introduction of comprehensive secondary education in Leek. The planned school merges with the nearby Westwood Hall High School and is opened as St Edward's Hall of the comprehensive Westwood County High School. There is a common timetable and interchange of staff. The new building is not handed over to the local authority and St Edward's remains a separate legal entity with its own board of governors.

Adams Butter Ltd goes public.

1966 – The Leek branch of the Samaritans is established and occupies a small room in Russell Street.

Each of the eight almhouses in Condlyffe Road are divided into an upper and a lower selfcontained flat.

Springhill hostel in Mount Road, for adults with learning difficulties, is opened.

Milward Hall in Salisbury Street is bought for the mortgage department of Leek and Westbourne Building Society.

The Adams Butter company's fleet of refrigerated vehicles is concentrated at a depot on an 11½-acre site at Barnfields.

Petty France is cleared.

1967 – At St Edward's Church, the mechanism of the 1874 clock is retained for the quarter and hour chimes when it is replaced by an electric clock.

East Street Primary School is extended, by the addition of an assembly hall.

Wardle and Davenport are suffering heavy losses.

Leek Chemicals becomes a subsidiary of Courtaulds. Sir Thomas and Arthur Wardle Ltd also becomes a subsidiary of Courtaulds.

1968 – Most of the buildings belonging to Brough, Nicholson and Hall, west of Cross Street, are demolished.

150th Anniversary of the founding of Anthony Ward & Co – first mill to be opened in Leek

No. 10 Stockwell Street is rented for the new computer department of Leek and Westbourne Building Society, which soon requires larger premises and moves to St Luke's church hall.

Hubert Newton of Leek and Westbourne Building Society is knighted.

The telephone exchange is replaced by a subscriber trunk dialling exchange on the site of the former Post Office in St Edward Street.

Most of the buildings west of Cross Street, including Hope Mill, are demolished.

The practise of having the Leek Mill Holiday on the first Monday in October lapses.

Weavers' cottages in Wood Street are demolished.

Hill Bros (Leek) Ltd., publishers of the *Leek Post and Times*, move into the former workhouse building in Brook Street being used as a dye-works.

At the West Street day school, numbers are reduced to 200 pupils.

1969 – Woodcroft County First School, Wallbridge Drive, is opened as a primary school, initially taking infants only.

The Lord's Prayer and Bible readings are introduced into Club Day.

Martins amalgamates with Barclays Bank Ltd.

The East Street Primary School annexe at St Luke's hall is closed with the opening of new schools in town, which has caused a steady reduction in numbers.

Haregate County Primary School, Churnet View opens.

1970 – Harold Davies loses at the election and is created a life peer as Baron Davies of Leek. The Conservative, David L. Knox, gains the seat.

The National Provincial Bank becomes part of National Westminster Bank Ltd.

The Leek and Moorlands Co-operative Society concentrates all trading on the department store in High Street.

The Westminster Bank Ltd branch is closed after the formation of National Westminster Bank.

The railway line from Leek to Leekbrook is closed.

Joshua Wardle Ltd switches its dyeing from 90 per cent woven fabrics to 90 per cent knitted.

Job White and Sons is acquired by Wardle and Davenport Ltd, which goes into liquidation later the same year.

Newton House is built on 27 acres on a landscaped site on the east side of Cheddleton Road as Leek and Westbourne Building Society's new headquarters. It is designed by Adams and Green of StokeonTrent. New Stockwell House is retained as the towncentre branch office.

There is only one firm still producing silk goods: Thomas Whittles Ltd, a family firm which operates at Wellington Mills in Strangman Street.

Wallbridge Park is extended.

1971 – The junior training centre becomes the Leek Day Special School and is soon afterwards renamed the Springfield Special School.

Stockwell Street fire station is replaced by a new station in Springfield Road.

The youth centre is opened in 1971 in Milward Hall in Salisbury Street, formerly part of Leek parish church school.

The population of Leek and Lowe is 19,452.

The new St Paul's Church is built in Novi Lane. The Church Commissioners make a grant of £15,000 towards the cost of building.

1972 – The Congregational Church becomes the Leek United Reformed Church.

Slum clearance in Mill Street is completed.

All of the buildings in Church Street, including both the George and the Golden Lion, are demolished for road widening. The Conservative Association clubhouse also goes.

A new house is built next door to the existing vicarage as a new vicarage for All Saints'.

Herbert Lisle is appointed OBE.

The Irish Dairy Board Cooperative Ltd, having acquired shares in Adams Butter in 1971, becomes the major shareholder and the company, with growing diversification of interests, is renamed Adams Foods Ltd.

The Leek Choral Society is founded under the direction of Keith Davis, choirmaster at Brunswick Methodist Church.

The Primitive Methodist Chapel in Fountain Street is demolished.

Martins Bank Leek branch closes.

John Myatt sells the printing business, which retains the name George Hill and Sons.

Brindley's Mill Trust formed to restore the mill.

Woodcroft County First School closed.

1973 – Leek railway station is demolished.

Belle Vue Mill is demolished, and a lingerie factory built on the site.

Most of the contents of the church library are sold.

1974 – Brindley's Mill is opened as a working mill and museum.

The nuns move from King Street to a smaller house in Alsop Street.

The Leek and Westbourne Building Society is merged with Ipswich-based Eastern Counties Building Society, which results in a further change of name, to the Leek and Westbourne and Eastern Counties Building Society.

The Urban District Council stops being an independent library authority. It is the smallest in Staffordshire when the library service is handed over to the County Council. The County Council also runs the museum and art gallery under an agency agreement with Staffordshire Moorlands District Council.

Land at Oulton, in Rushton Spencer, purchased for charitable purposes, is sold.

The former urban district becomes a parish in the Staffordshire Moorlands district, with a town council of twelve members representing four wards and its chairman designated the mayor of Leek. The parish is represented on the District Council by twelve members.

The Pride of the Moorlands Lodge of the Order of Sisters becomes part of Unity's Loyal Westwood Lodge.

Wall Bridge Farm is demolished and also an area of the pre1934 sewage farm.

The Staffordshire Moorlands District is centred on Leek. The Council Offices are at New Stockwell House in Stockwell Street and in the Town Hall in Market Street as well as Moorlands House off Stockwell Street.

The Jehovah's Witnesses meetings are revived using a room in Ashbourne Road.

The congregations of Mount Pleasant and Brunswick use their chapels for joint services on alternate Sundays.

The Leek and Westbourne and Eastern Counties Building Society merges with the Oldbury Britannia Building Society and becomes the Britannia Building Society.

1975 – Bread is still being left in the porch of St Edward's Church for collection by poor (see 1822).

Fish in the Leek to Cheddleton stretch of the River Churnet are wiped out in a spillage.

The swimming pool is opened in Brough Park.

Adams Foods Ltd, the largest butter-selling organisation in the United Kingdom, opens its warehouse and cold storage plant on the Barnfields industrial estate.

The water supply to the Challinor Fountain in Brough Park is cut off because the fountain is being vandalised.

The Maude Institute is altered and enlarged.

Flowers, shrubs and trees are planted in Mill Street.

1976 – The Samaritans move to Fountain Street.

A scheme defines the potential beneficiaries of the Milner Bequest as persons living in Leek or attending an educational establishment there.

A new house is built in Novi Lane for the vicar of St Luke's Church.

The congregations of Mount Pleasant and Brunswick unite as the Central Methodist Church, continuing to use both chapels.

The Brunswick chapel is closed.

The Britannia Building Society sells New Stockwell House to the Staffordshire Moorlands District Council, a branch office having been opened in Derby Street.

The County Council's offices, which occupy much of the site of Brough, Nicholson and Hall in Cross Street, are opened.

1977 – The Brunswick School in Regent Street is demolished.

The united congregations of the Mount Pleasant and Brunswick chapels amalgamate with Leek United Reformed Church to form the Trinity Church, using the United Reformed Church building in Derby Street.

A week of concerts and other entertainments is organised which leads to the establishment of the Leek Arts Festival.

Squash courts are opened in Brough Park Leisure Centre.

1978 – Leek Arts Festival begins.

The Pentecostalists' present church in Buxton Road is built.

Ray Poole sells the printing side of the business to John Hilton.

The Irish Dairy Board Cooperative becomes the owner of Adams Foods Ltd.

Two industrial estates are developed at Leekbrook and Barnfields.

1979 – The old public baths are demolished.

The former National Westminster Bank building becomes a community centre occupied by the Citizens' Advice Bureau and voluntary services.

The Mount Road reservoir is demolished as the water undertaking is now owned by Severn Trent Water Limited.

All Saints' and St Luke's parishes becomes part of the new parish of Leek, with its vicar becoming a team vicar in a team ministry composed of the rector and two vicars. The existing vicar of St Edward's is named as the first team rector and the vicars of All Saints' and St Luke's as first team vicars. Thereafter the rector is to be appointed by the Leek Patronage Board, consisting of the bishop, the archdeacon of StokeuponTrent, and three members chosen by the parochial church council of Leek parish. The vicars are to be appointed by the bishop and the rector jointly.

1980 – The nuns continue to teach at both Roman Catholic schools until they leave Leek during this year.

The Mount Pleasant chapel is demolished, and sheltered flats are opened on the site.

The Seventh Day Adventists start to hold services in a private house.

The Staffordshire Moorlands District Council takes direct control of the museum exhibits and most of the paintings are put into store.

The Britannia Building Society extends Newton House.

Numerous textile mills are closing.

Leek's first housingassociation project, Westwood Court in North Street, is opened, providing sheltered accommodation for older people. Built by Anchor Housing Association they consist of nineteen single flats, nine for two persons, and three for three persons.

The Scheme for the almshouses built at the corner of Broad Street and Compton restricts almswomen to residents of an area within five miles of Leek Market Place, preference being given to those living in one of the former townships of ancient parish, and is renamed Ash Homes.

John Hilton sells the printing business in Getliffe Yard to Getliffe Design and Print.

The Britannia Building Society replace the branch office in Derby Street with a new building on the site of the baths on the corner of Derby Street and Bath Street.

1981 – Leek is one of the areas in which the County Council adopts a threetier system of schools, involving first schools for children under the age of nine, middle schools for children aged nine to thirteen, and High School s for children aged thirteen to eighteen.

The Haregate County Primary School is closed and the building is taken over by the new Churnet View Middle School and extended.

All Saints' C.E. School becomes a first school.

The Leek United Reformed Church is reordered internally, the organ being rebuilt with parts from an organ in Brunswick Methodist chapel, and space under the gallery converted into a vestibule.

Woodcroft County First School becomes a first school. Threetier schooling is introduced. The number of children on the school's roll is reduced to 1,000, and the school is concentrated at Springfield Road, where the buildings are extended. The Westwood Road buildings become St Edward's middle school. Westwood Hall becomes the school's Old Hall and the former St Edward's building its New Hall.

St. Paul's School, Novi Lane becomes a first school.

Churnet view, the County Middle School, is opened in the former Haregate County Primary School. the building being modified and extended.

The unusual status of a voluntary aided school being also part of a maintained school continues until a further reorganisation of Leek schools. The St Edward's Hall building is then handed over to the County Council for use by Westwood High School The governors of St Edward's Hall receive in exchange Leek High School's Warrington Hall building, which is opened that year as St Edward's C.E. (Aided) Middle School.

The Carr Trust is formed by the amalgamation of the charities of Charles Carr, William Carr and Elizabeth Flint. Charles Carr (d. 1888) had left interest on £1,250 to be spent on the poor living in Leek town or within five miles.

The Scheme for the Carr Almshouses in Fountain Street renames the charity "Carr Homes".

East Street becomes a first school.

The College of Further Education and School of Art and Crafts are combined to form Leek College of Further Education and School of Art. There are annexes in Union Street and Russell Street.

West Street Day School becomes a first school and numbers drop to 100.

St Luke's School is closed.

St Luke's Church Infants' School in Queen Street is closed and becomes a parish hall.

The population of Leek and Lowe is 19,724.

1982 – Part of Wardle's premises are taken over by Courtaulds Jersey.

The Seventh Day Adventists transfer their services to the Friends' Meeting House.

1983 – The parish of Meerbrook is added to Leek, which becomes the parish of Leek and Meerbrook.

The Leek and District Manufacturers' and Dyers' Association, with its membership declining, is dissolved.

The Cross Street Mill is taken over by Berisfords, a Congleton ribbon firm.

West Street Day School closes.

1984 – Leek and District Historical Society is formed.

A performing arts studio is opened in what had once been Westwood Hall's banqueting room.

A.J. Worthington (Holdings) Ltd announces heavy losses, partly as a result of the closure of its subsidiary.

Another large housing scheme is the Beth Johnson Housing Association's sheltered housing, opened on a site off the Mount Pleasant Methodist Chapel in Clerk Bank, and consisting of thirty-one single flats and eight double.

Leek and Moorlands Co-operative Society's department store in High Street is replaced by a superstore opened by North Midland Cooperative Society Ltd in Pickwood Road, for which much of the area west of Pickwood Road is cleared.

1985 – Plans for the redevelopment of the area on the east side of the Market Place are put in hand and the District Council invites proposals

A separate building comprising four flats for additional almswomen is built in Compton on the south side of the almshouses by Basil Bailey of Cheadle.

The Grand Theatre closes.

1986 – A sports hall is built in Brough Park.

Turnover at Worthingtons increases with the reemergence of White and Sons, and the company shows a profit again.

The Trustee Savings Bank is opened in Market Place.

The former Cooperative Society store on the corner of High Street and Field Street is converted into a Court House for the Magistrates' Court.

The Market Cross is moved back to the Market Square.

Leek College of Further Education and School of Art's technology block and business studies centre is opened in Union Street, as well as a subsidiary centre for further education at Biddulph.

1987 – The former pastor of the Buxton Road Pentecostalist church establishes a separate congregation called Oasis Ministries in the former Methodist school in West Street.

The Regal Bingo Hall at the corner of High Street and Salisbury Street is closed, taken over by Jehovah's Witnesses as their Kingdom Hall.

East Street Primary School has 200 on the roll.

Joshua Wardle Ltd is bought by a major customer, William Baird plc.

The new council offices are opened.

1988 – Fred Hill's bookshop is closed.

Most of the original hospital buildings on the west side of Ashbourne Road are demolished.

The council chamber is added to the civic offices.

Cross Street Mill is converted into an antiques showroom.

A largescale antiques trade develops, with showrooms and warehouses occupying converted buildings such as Cross Street Mill and Compton School.

The Challinor Fountain is moved to the forecourt of Moorlands House in Stockwell Street.

Leek and District Historical Society publishes a journal called *Chronicles*.

Bethesda Chapel is demolished.

The present Leek Baptist Church is built on site of Emmanuel Baptist Church in Rosebank Street.

One of the mills formerly belonging to Brough, Nicholson and Hall is turned into an antiques showroom.

The town hall is demolished, and the town council's offices are moved to 15 Stockwell Street.

A scheme for the east side of Market Place is finally adopted, despite strong opposition.

Leonard Street police station is replaced by one in Fountain Street.

Leekensian Amateur Operatic Society performances are given in Trinity Church in Derby Street.

Of 851 hectares in Leek civil parish, 732 hectares are grassland, 73 hectares are rough grazing, and 42 hectares are woodland. There are 1,869 head of cattle, including calves, and 444 sheep, including 204 breeding ewes and 212 lambs. Of the thirty-five holdings returned, there are eleven fulltime farms, ten of them entirely devoted to dairying and others mainly so. All are under 100 hectares in size, with only five of 50 hectares or more.

The Leek College of Further Education and School of Art, one of the smallest in North Staffordshire and serving Staffordshire Moorlands, has 260 fulltime students, 848 parttime day students, 117 parttime day and evening students, and 1,740 students taking evening classes.

1989 – The Irish Dairy Board Co-operative (owners of Adams Foods Ltd) is taken over by another subsidiary of the Cooperative, Kerrygold Co. Ltd.

Members of Leek and District Historical Society are involved in the establishment of Leek and Moorlands Historical Trust, one of whose aims is the opening of a heritage centre in the town.

The railway lines from Leekbrook to Cauldon and to Stoke, serving Caldon Low limestone quarries, are closed.

Good fishing returns to the River Churnet between Leek and Cheddleton. The National Rivers Authority releases over 2,000 chub and dace into the river and answers fears about their survival by stating that the dye-works effluent is harmless and that the only danger is from the Leekbrook sewage works.

1990 – The income of the Town Lands Trust amounts to £7,334, derived from the rent of Dee Bank farm and from investments; £5,340 is spent on donations, mainly to local organisations, income having to be used for the benefit of the inhabitants of Leek and Lowe.

A floor is inserted in the tower of St Edward's Church to create a meeting room which extends under the west gallery and over the parlour. A kitchen and lavatory are inserted on the ground floor of the tower.

The Beth Johnson Association completes the first phase of forty pensioners' flats in Pickwood Close.

The Moorside Youth Centre in the grounds of Leek High School is opened.

The Mill Street Wesleyan School ceases to be used as a chapel.

St Edward's Hall has 700 on the roll.

After being refurbished and extended, the Moorlands Hospital is opened as a community hospital, and the cottage hospital and the Salisbury Street clinic are closed.

Houses are built over the Beggars Lane cricket ground but the Highfield ground continues in use.

A Safeway superstore is opened on the site of the railway station.

Leek Arts Festival lasts for four weeks.

Leek Town FC club is the losing finalist at Wembley for the Football Association Challenge Trophy.

A board is unveiled in St Edward's Church commemorating airmen who have been killed.

Mill Street Chapel and Ragged School is closed.

1991 – Much of the income of the Carr Trust is spent on payments of £10 month to some 100 persons, who also receive a £20 Christmas bonus in the form of parcels or vouchers to old people at Christmas.

There is a distribution of c. £950 from combined funds of all charities included in the Town Dole, given in small cash payments to individuals and families in need, distributed by the warden of Leek in consultation with social agencies.

Four other charities, originally administered separately, have been incorporated into Town Dole. James Rudyard's charity is administered by the warden of Leek, together with those of John Rothwell and John Naylor.

St Luke's Players are renamed Leek Players.

The population of Leek and Lowe is 19,518.

The former St Mary's Church, which was being used as a parish hall, has stood empty for several years.

Kerrygold opens its United Kingdom headquarters in Sunnyhill Road, Barnfields. There is also a cheesepacking plant built there and another for processed cheese. The Springfield Road site is put up for sale.

The foundry of Sneyd Engineering Co. Ltd closes with the loss of some sixteen jobs.

At the local elections, the Ratepayers group wins a number of seats on both the parish and district councils.

1992 – Leek College of Further Education and School of Art buys the Carr Gymnasium, adjoining the Nicholson Institute, from the District Council.

The Milward Hall Youth and Community Centre is used by all age groups.

The Springfield Special School has thirty places and takes children aged two to nineteen with severe learning difficulties or physical disabilities.

The largest employer in town is the Britannia Building Society.

eriLusta is at Big Mill, but has to lose forty members of its workforce of ninety when it moves to premises in Belle Vue Road.

Leek's importance as a centre for production of knitted goods continues to grow. It is estimated that 75 per cent of the knitted scarves worn in Britain are made in the town.

The Albion Mill is turned into an animal foods plant.

At St Edward's Hall a new wing is opened.

he Britannia Building Society opens Britannia House, on the opposite side of Cheddleton road from Newton House.

Leek has two lodges of Freemasons, St Edward's and DieuLaCresse.

The Leek Central Liberal Club continues to function as a social club called Leek Central Club.

Leek has about a dozen textile firms, involved mainly in dyeing, finishing, printing and production of knitwear, braids and trimmings.

The Leek and District Fly Fishing Club secures an outof-court settlement from Severn Trent Water for the loss of fishing rights in the river between Kingsley and Alton since 1984 as a result of pollution from the sewage works. New treatment processes are completed designed to produce an improvement in the effluent discharged into the river.

There are four packaging firms in the town.

The Maude Institute is used by various voluntary organisations.

Leek May Fair ends.

Quaker Meetings for worship are still being held.

The Pump Street mission church building survives as a Boy Scout headquarters.

The style "Queen of the Moorlands" is used on signs erected on the five roads entering the town.

Improvements at Leekbrook introduce sewage treatment processes claimed to be unique in Europe outside Italy.

David Knox is elected as Leek's MP for the seventh time.

A smaller industrial estate is developed in Station Street on the former town yard.

Westwood Golf Club clubhouse, designed by David Horne of GCW Architects of StokeonTrent, is opened.

Milk Street Church at Ball Haye Green remains open for worship.

The income of the church trust, some £50 a year, is spent on books for use by the clergy of the team rectory.

The last performance by the operatic society established at All Saints' Church takes place. There are no more because of the lack of a suitable public hall for largescale productions following the demolition of the Town Hall in 1988.

Unity's Loyal Westwood Lodge becomes an independent club called the Leek Westwood Friendly Society,

Brunswick Mill is being converted into flats.

The income from Ann Jolliffe's charity (see 1732) sees a distribution of £35 made to thirty-nine Leek widows.

The Milner Bequest charity's income, £3,500, is distributed mainly in interestfree loans to college and university students and in grants for pupils to study and travel in Great Britain and abroad in pursuit of their education.

1993 – Beth Johnson Association completes the scheme in Pickwood Close.

The Leek College of Further Education and School of Art becomes selfmanaging, and responsibility for funding it passes from the County Council to the Further Education Funding Council for England.

The Post Office is replaced by a post office in part of the premises of Genies Lighting in Haywood Street.

David L. Knox MP is knighted.

1994 – Springhill hostel in Mount Road, for adults with learning difficulties, houses thirty-one people.

Horsecroft Grove, consisting of ten bungalows built by a housing association, is opened.

The plate at St Edward's Church includes a 14th century silvergilt North German chalice and a silver Swiss chalice dated 1641, both given in 1912 by Mrs Barron (nee Gaunt), plus two silver chalices and patens of 1777, one of the patens being the gift of Thomas Higginbotham, and a flagon of 1777 inscribed as the gift of F.M. There is also a wooden cross which belonged to the Emperor Maximilian of Mexico, which is inlaid with mother of pearl and inset with a reputed relic of the True Cross. The church also possesses several pieces of Leek embroidery, including three frontals designs respectively by Gerald Horsley, J.D. Sedding and R. Norman Shaw.

The former St Marys Church, used as parish hall, has stood empty for several years, and burns down.

At the Leek College of Further Education and School of Art, the interior of the 1900 building is remodelled to provide more study space and better reception facilities.

An outdoor Saturday market specialising in crafts and antiques begins.

The new scheme for the Market Place is still under consideration.

There are three general markets per week and two cattle markets being held in Leek.

Leek becomes United Kingdom headquarters of Kerrygold Co. Ltd, the dairy products firm which has taken over Adams Butter.

A Monday cattle market specialising in calves starts following the closure of the Smithfield at NewcastleunderLyme.

A nursery class is opened at All Saints' C.E. School.

Thomas Whittles Ltd ceases to operate, and the silk industry in Leek comes to an end.

1996 – The Memorial to the French POWs is erected.